From

Letters
to
Leaders:

Creating Impact on Your
College Campus and Beyond

By

**Michael Ayalon and the
Greek University Team**

Copyright © 2021 Michael Ayalon and the Greek University Team

All rights reserved.
No part of this publication may be reproduced, distributed or
transmitted in any form or by any means, including photocopying,
recording or other electronic or mechanical methods, without the
prior written permission of the publisher, except in the case of brief
quotations, reviews and other noncommercial uses permitted by
copyright law.

Contents

Introduction

Michael Ayalon

Our fraternities and sororities, and specifically our Ritual, should serve as our lifetime roadmap for values, ethics, morals, and beliefs. Where can one learn more about these guiding lights? For me, it was first taught to me by my parents, my teachers, my religion, and then by my fraternity. They are all connected.

My father always taught me respect for others, especially my elders. Violence of any kind was never tolerated. He always believed that only a fool would act out physically against another human being, as he felt that any dispute could be resolved through proper discussion and compromise. The only acceptable form of violence in his mind was self-defense. Anything other than that was completely unacceptable in our household, and this mantra was repeated over and over to me throughout my childhood.

The Jewish people are full of pride. There is an expectation that one would marry another Jewish person and start having many Jewish children. It is a form of self-preservation, especially after so many members of our family died in the Holocaust. Luckily, my grandparents managed to escape Nazi concentration camps, and they passed on to their children their strong belief in Judaism, as well as the principles and values that go with it. Since my immediate family was living in New York, away from all of our extended family in Israel (including aunts, uncles, and cousins), they decided to send me to a private Hebrew day school. This way I would stay in touch with my faith. I attended Solomon Schechter for eight years, from 1st through 8th grade. The curriculum there is a mix of modern and timeless, in that half the day would be spent on twenty-first-century skills, and the other half of the day would be spent learning classical Jewish values through study of the Hebrew language, the Torah, and the Talmud. The values that were taught to us include a love of Israel, social action, respect, community, lifelong learning, and observance.

Our teachers were a mix of modern and classic, depending on the subject being taught. Any class on the Torah or the Talmud was certainly taught by a Rabbi, as he had the familiarity and the credibility to lead such a discussion. The discussion on respect always seemed to be a focus for every Rabbi who taught us through those eight years. We spent a significant amount of time on the Ten Commandments, and I remember "Honor thy father and thy mother" was a major discussion. Striking or cursing a parent was punishable by death, which seemed to be excessive to me at the time. In the Talmud, there is a comparison between honoring one's parents to honoring God. Interestingly enough, Assault and Battery is something covered in the Talmud, and in those times the discussion focused on compensation for the person who was hurt, not necessarily in terms of the punishment. There is a section that deals with an "eye for an eye," but the interpretation is monetary compensation, it does not mean the infliction of similar pain. Needless to say, respect for others was a focus in our curriculum, and this religious foundation repeats itself over and over again throughout my studies in Judaism as a child.

After eight years in a private school, I felt that it was time to make the transition to a public high school. Making that transition was difficult. When I graduated high school, I had to make a decision on where I was going for college. At this point, my neighborhood friend Scott was already attending college at the University at Buffalo. I had never been to Buffalo before, but I committed to the University, sight unseen, because of my relationship with Scott. I called Scott a week before my freshman year at college. I could not wait to start this new stage of life in college with all the freedom and opportunity that it represented. When I finally reached Scott, he told me he had some bad news. Scott explained that he got a job as a security guard and he worked all night long, so he wasn't able to wake up for his morning classes throughout his freshman year. Scott explained that he failed out, and now I would be heading to Buffalo by myself. How could this happen? Now I was starting all over again.

The ride from the New York City area where I grew up was about eight hours to Buffalo. When I finally arrived after the long trip, I received the keys to my dorm room, and then proceeded to my room. Buffalo has amazing chicken wings, and my favorite was the Buffalo Chicken Finger Sub. The amazing smells coming from the student dining hall in the basement of the building could attract me all the way from my dorm room. I did find comfort in the food (and easily put on well more weight than the usual freshman fifteen), but close friends were much harder to come by. Everywhere I turned, it seemed as if every other student among the 30,000 students enrolled was best friends with the roommate they were assigned to. They would be going to the gym together, eating together, and engaging in social activities together. I had trouble interfacing with 30,000 students. It was overwhelming, and I didn't know where to begin. The first semester at school I was always doing one of three things: eating, sleeping, and going to class. There was no social life, and as we got closer to the end of my first semester, I had arrived at the decision that college wasn't for me.

I took my phone outside of my dorm room, I sat down on the floor in the hallway, and then I called my father. I told him that I had given this much thought, and I had decided to drop out of college and start my career without a college degree. My father hesitated for a minute, which felt like five minutes for me, and then said with absolute certainty that his son was going to be a college graduate. Even after I explained that I didn't want to be there, he indicated that returning home was not an option (in very colorful language).

I was now sitting in Calculus class in my second semester. It was January in Buffalo. There was five feet of snow on the ground outside, and it was still snowing. I looked to my left, and there was a student sitting next to me wearing cut-off jean shorts and flip-flops to class! What was he thinking leaving the house dressed like that? As I shook my head in disbelief, I noticed a tattoo of Greek letters on his thigh. I wondered why anyone in their right mind would agree to put an organization on their thigh so they can look at it every day. I remember thinking, *This must have been the greatest organization on the planet!* After class, I pulled him aside, and asked him about it. He introduced himself as Rich, and he said that he could tell me about the founders of the organization as well as its history, but it would be easier if I just followed him to the fraternity house and meet all the members. Lucky for him, my social calendar was clear.

I met the fraternity brothers and thought they were a nice bunch of guys, but that's about it. I returned home that day, eager to see what the next few days would bring. When I returned to Calculus class two days later, I sat next to Rich again. After class, Rich asked if I could come with him back to the fraternity house again. After checking my non-existent social calendar, I agreed to go. This time, when I got to the house, they all greeted me. "It's great to see you again, Mike. Thanks for coming by."

They knew my name! They actually missed me if I didn't stop by the house. I had a family again, for the first time in a long time. I decided to join the organization, and they handed me a manual to study. Upon opening the manual, I read the creed of the fraternity. It talked about fellowship, brotherhood, truth, justice, scholarship, chivalry, culture, character, and service. I really liked these new friends that

I made, and their organization has the same ethics and character that I had growing up, the same values that I was taught by my parents, by my teachers, and by my religion. It was precisely what I had been looking for, and the brothers were the connection I needed in order to be successful at college. Not only would they be my brothers in an unfamiliar environment, but they would tutor me in the classes I needed help in, they would guide me to take classes and learn from professors that would work to my strengths. The fraternity would give me immediate leadership opportunities to help build an organization of men who were going to change the world for the better. I was in for the ride.

The pledging process took sixty days. I learned the material in the pledge manual, I knew the creed of the fraternity, I knew all the letters of the Greek alphabet, and I knew all of my new brothers. They were a diverse group of men from all over the country. We were the misfits of sorts, mostly because nobody on campus could tell you what a typical brother looked like in our chapter. There was a jock fraternity full of athletes, there was another fraternity full of men that took an hour of prep time to get ready each morning, but none like us. We seemingly had a member of every race, color, religion, country of origin, and sexual orientation. Our group wore that as a badge of honor, and they would explain that every time someone inquired on why they should join our organization. It made us better. Even at the initial meetings that I was attending during pledging, you could see that they looked at problems from so many different points of view, each of them bringing their own experiences to the table in making judgments, and they came out of the meeting unified in whatever decision the group made. This democracy within the fraternity was one of the most appealing parts of the organization. I now had a healthy fascination with *Robert's Rules of Order.*

While we certainly had our share of problems in our chapter, we worked together to build the best organization on our campus. We recruited new leadership, improved our scholarship initiatives, and started to really live the values of the organization instead of just saying them. We discussed the values of the organization at the conclusion of our weekly meetings, and we showed how the actions of a particular brother matched the values of the organization that week. It was a way for us to reaffirm our beliefs, morals, and values to each other every single week. I went on to take leadership roles that I never would have felt comfortable taking prior to being in the fraternity. I was Fundraising Chairman my freshman year, Social Chairman my sophomore year, Treasurer my junior year, and President of the chapter in my senior year. I learned leadership skills and communication skills that are just not offered in the classroom.

Where else on campus could you manage a big budget and handle accounts receivable and accounts payable while still in college? Where else could you learn to motivate dozens of college students who each have their own direction in life, but with strong leadership, get them all to work together toward a common cause or purpose? Where else could you learn public speaking skills on a weekly basis in front of a group of your peers? How about accountability mechanisms such as a judicial board to keep your members in line with the values of the fraternity? How about a sense of civic duty, to leave this community that we live in a better place? Event planning? Fundraising in the community? I essentially ran a business while in college. It would pay huge dividends in the future for me. I had a leg up on many other college graduates who never had that experience, and that's the reason why I'm so passionate about fraternity and sorority life today. I firmly believe that fraternities and sororities are the best leadership experience on a college campus. However, as we can see from the headlines in newspapers across the country, when it's done wrong, it can lead to disaster.

Decades later, I would spend some time working as the Executive Director of the same fraternity I joined in college. During this span of over three years at headquarters, I visited many of our chapters all across North America. I would see recurring problems on most of the campuses that I would visit, including problems such as alcohol and drug abuse, sexual assaults, and hazing on these campuses. On September 15, 2015, I read an article in the *New York Times* that discussed five members of another fraternity at Baruch College who were being charged with murder in a 2013 fraternity hazing incident. As a parent, I could not imagine the pain and anger they must have felt when their son died. We must protect our members and guests at all times. Our brothers and sisters should be in the best position to do just that when the members of our organization are living the values of our organization. I wanted to get on the road and start working with members of every fraternity, every sorority, on every college campus in North America to help make it safer. Greek University immediately started in September of 2015 with presentations and workshops for Greek communities. It was only me. It was difficult to keep on top of all the issues given the number of fraternity/sorority communities all over the country, and we needed a diverse set of professionals. I could not be the expert at everything, and we needed more hands.

Over time, we recruited the best professionals in the industry to help fraternity and sorority members with other problems in addition to risk management concerns. We brought on new professionals to help with diversity, equity, and inclusion, and have had success working with national headquarters on high-level diversity initiatives. We brought on fraternity/sorority recruitment experts and mental health advocates. Our speaking professionals now work on topics such as empathy, healthy relationships, emotional intelligence, vulnerability, fundraising, healthy masculinity, motivation, and much more. The impact on our campuses has been substantial, and this new organization we created reflected my values. We have helped our chapters grow, made our campuses safer, and inspired college students all over North America by initiating the following actions:

- provide these engaging and interactive presentations
- leverage social media
- build a podcast full of expert interviews
- enhance student skills
- provide mentoring/coaching
- improve existing systems
- change consequences for actions (incentives/disincentives) with real accountability
- improve the physical design of our campus environments

- change policies in our communities and organizations

Without fail, former students find us at the major industry conferences where we speak. The best reward is hearing about all the new initiatives that were implemented following one of our visits and the measurable success they are seeing. The last five years have been life-changing for our team and our students.

I'm so proud of what our team has become on this journey. I am so humbled to work with such an immensely talented group of people at Greek University. Not only do we have shared values and beliefs, but our team is also really talented at what they do and they get the desired results on the campuses they visit. This team motivates me to work harder every single day—they make me a better person, a better father, and a better husband. By introducing them to you here and on our website, it is my hope that you will invite them to your campus so they can motivate you to be the best chapter, best council, and best community you can be. Let your values guide you and the organization. Not just today, but over your entire journey called life. I believe in our fraternities and sororities to make this world a better place, and most of all, I believe in you.

When people are afraid or defensive, they have no tolerance for the person at the edge of inside. They want purity, rigid loyalty, and lock step unity. But now more than ever we need people who have the courage to live on the edge of inside, who love their parties and organizations so much that they can critique them as a brother, operate on them from the inside as a friend and dauntlessly insist that they live up to their truest selves. —David Brooks

Michael can be reached by email at: bookings@greekuniversity.org

The website is: www.greekuniversity.org

CHAPTER 1

Follow the Beat of Your Own Drum

Mel Lewis

While the title of this chapter is quite cheesy, the content is meant to provide a place of understanding and possibility. We are strangers together in this second sentence, unfamiliar with each other's comfort zones. Where you have been, before reading this, is unique to you, and where I am writing this is a coffee shop on the Jersey Shore—we are of the same in mind, I just might be more caffeinated. So, let me set the precedent in saying this is meant to be a safe space where I will share myself with you, you will digest it, and process it in your own way. The topic is growth and how we embrace it or are ignorant to it. Now, let's begin!

I always believed myself to be self-assured throughout my life: I knew I was an awkward height and weight, I was considered a funny person, and I thrived in busy and loud environments. I could be overly gregarious, and I wasn't the best academically; I had a multitude of different circles and even did a great attempt at having a dating life. I was riding a slightly above average reality until I experienced college and with its new opportunities and different people. I had realized that there had been a fog that had followed me throughout life that made its presence either a dull buzz or an overpowering roar. The fog had two heads: Depression and Anxiety; it decided to darken the skies or to awaken storms that I was never given the tools to ride or fight. The worst part about the fog was that others couldn't see it for what it was and would question its existence. It was easier for me to become the sun and keep the fog and its effects on me hidden. Fake it till you make it, as they say.

In 2010, I was a sophomore at college experiencing the phenomenon known as the "Sophomore Slumps." I questioned who I was and if my current existence could endure. Prior to that year, my college experience has been wonderful; I had made a strong group of friends quickly, I was close enough to home, and I was able to attend new types of events.

I did not expect the fog to become stronger in silence while I navigated this new world, but I was wrong.

I want to be as transparent as possible with you, reader: just because someone does not have a plan to end their life, does not negate their fear to exist. The numbness that surrounded this feeling was isolating; the sun I had created to shield others was weakening. The girl who I was—confused and battling the fog—desperately searched for a smidge of light in different clubs and organizations, risky parties, and overindulging in food. The unexpected shimmer of hope came on a cold day in January 2011 from a Southern woman dressed in red and wearing a welcoming smile who was sitting at a lone table in my college's cafeteria. She was there to discuss a new opportunity that was being brought to our campus: a new chapter of an international sorority.

Yes, a twenty-two-year-old leadership consultant who wanted to recruit close to one hundred women from New Jersey to start a commonly known Southern sorority was the beacon of light that I did not know that I needed.

The minimal knowledge I had about sororities was that they embodied everything that I was not. I could confidently tell you that I did not even know what groups were on my campus or what they did, just that I occasionally saw students in matching block-lettered windbreakers who would travel in packs. I shared classes with them, lived in residence halls, and even had a few friends who wore all different letters; it was always something that I placed into a box with restricted barriers. What I was really doing was placing myself into boxes that I have been comfortable with my whole life.

I thought that my world was binary and there was little else to be learned—boy, was I incredibly wrong. I had multiple boxes to my identity instead of flowing through different possibilities that could open me up to myself. This is where so many have unknowingly created restrictions on growth for themselves and others, basing internal identities upon external factors.

Let's unpack that together, shall we?

To document my experience starting a chapter of a sorority with ninety other women who were practically strangers, creating a self-governing structure, and all the additional nooks-and-crannies would exceed the length restrictions of this chapter. The aspects of this journey, however, are crucial to include because they exemplify the external and internal barriers of growth. I will say it loud and proud here: I am a sorority woman who exceeds all expectations while inspiring ambition. This part of my identity is not something I would have ever thought possible prior to meeting the consultant, interviewing for membership, and engaging in the experience. I'm not sure I would have even considered this title while learning about sisterhood, service, autonomy, and unity. I can, however, confidently pinpoint the moment I was certain I was a sorority woman: it was during my last recruitment preference ceremony where my senior speech started with the words that are now the title of this chapter. The lesson is not in that journey, but in the realization that others had not considered me for the opportunity to hold that identity and claim its box.

No need to feel sorry for me here, reader; I have been out of college for some time now. My focus is on the college students of today who wear the block letters and hold the membership that are losing sight of others' identities and potential because they cannot understand their own. How many students have been neglected because they do not fit inside a box; why are we not talking about the fluidity of identity and how it deserves our utmost attention?

These are not bold questions that I stumbled upon while an undergraduate member and possibly not even while I was well into my graduate program, earning my master's degree in student affairs. Heck, it might not even have been until I was working on college campuses with students that I understood how unique my collegiate experience had been. That is when I started to analyze my world prior to being affiliated.

Like I stated, I knew who I was at that point in my life. When I started the process of learning about my sorority and the education that surrounded it, I clung to those identifiers; not because they were comfortable, but because they were accepted and appreciated. There's this thing in Greek Life called Ritual and it is the purpose, the why, and the core of any organization. When I was initiated and exposed to my organization's Ritual, I can truthfully say that I was overcome with a plethora of emotions because I felt as if I had lived the words and meaning of our Ritual for my entire life. I learned that I had always been an amazing sorority member and now I was able to only develop further as a woman and person in my community.

So, if I was able to understand that my strengths and attributes were already exemplifying the core of a sorority member within a few hours, then how come others did not view me in that way for over a year that I was on that college campus? Why did other members of the community shake their head and roll their eyes when I started taking on leadership positions and raising important questions about the policies and procedures of this community that I had recently joined? I found the answer in a few comments from friends and family at home when they uncomfortably exclaimed a simple, yet powerful sentence: "You don't seem like a sorority girl." While their intention might have been to point out that I did not possess the "negative" stigmas, I only heard that I was not capable of the positives. I started to pick apart the boxes I had known about myself with doubt: was I too poor, too wide, not into makeup or hair product enough; was I not feminine enough to pass for someone that held the title of sorority member?

To be fair, these thoughts did not live in my heart while I was a collegiate member—what did the questions of a few mean to me when I had the support of so many in this new experience? These sisters saw and welcomed the fog that had tortured me, and taught me to accept the gray skies while reinventing the light. The brothers from the fraternities became my protectors in all situations instead of clinging to the role of a simple bystander. The community welcomed my ideas, my stories, and my laughter while teaching me to learn about diversity, problem solving, and crisis management. The sisters of the community were the ones I felt most at home with and the brothers were where I felt safest. I have mentioned my experience might have been unique because I do not hear of many similar scenarios today from fraternity and sorority members.

It resonated with me—the college student of today's reality versus the one that I had personally lived. In the position that I was in my career, I had the opportunity to educate and facilitate change, but where was I to begin? There had been so much I had been lucky to be exposed to as a leader about values—where I could unhinge my boxes of identity factors and become open to others and more fluid with my own. Where was I to begin in waking up a community of conditioned young adults to the reality of their power, privilege, and opportunities?

What I'm about to say goes against conventional wisdom, and others have a different view: From only my experience, a rule of mine is that I do not identify a problem without seeking out a solution first.

If you need to envision me writing "people are complex . . ." on a dry erase board and then underlining ". . . and need to be respected," then I encourage you to do so, reader. The solution I sought is that there are different levels of understanding growth, and it is a slow and steady journey. There is no identical method or reception to lessons or life, even when we expect there to be.

As previously stated, I immediately felt connected to my sorority Ritual ceremony and its meaning, while another sister needed additional time for reflection in order to connect with it. After careful consideration, this sister exclaimed, "I cannot wait to learn more now!" Back then, I thought it was bizarre that I could be so sure about something, while others had a completely different perception. Now, I am a bit less dramatic and can see the situations for what they are: in need of an individualistic approach.

Everyone is the expert of their own life; from their thoughts and their heart, they can speak the most honestly to their experience. If this is the case, then why do we expect others to mold into our ideologies without question? To really understand others, we must be opened to learning about them. When others do not agree with us, there tends to be more of a pull to understanding their "why not" instead of understanding their "why." This can also be true for when we do not agree with others; we can understand where we stand in that situation and choose to not be swayed in any other direction.

This is not a chapter about everyone agreeing and singing around a campfire (sorry to disappoint!); this is an aid to realize that everyone, including yourself, has lived a unique life prior to your meeting.

First, it is important to create a space that is going to aid in assessing your boxes, your goals, and your plans. This space may be difficult to create, but it is the place you will learn and feel validated. Lay out the different aspects of your identity: write it down on a list or post them up on the walls. If we think about each identity as a part of our story, we can appreciate how each element has its own importance. This is usually a bit easier for individuals, especially college students, to sit with since they have been in the same environment for their whole life until they enter a new community and a new world.

Before entering a new chapter and space, what do you think would be different about your life if one of your boxes was eliminated? How would your story be impacted if one of those boxes was changed? It's okay to admit that is an uncomfortable challenge to ponder; the whole point of growth is to learn what we do not know.

Second, it's important to know that these boxes aren't as restrictive as you may have conditioned yourself to believe. I know for me, my views of who I was that my boxes were set on only had potential to rise upward and linear. I know you do not know me all too well, but I am anything but linear. Something that college and my sorority experience taught me was that if you are open to learn about others, you will learn more about yourself. I could feel more confident with certain boxes, while questioning the privilege in other ones. The best way I was able to learn about my own identity was gaining new experiences—through unexpected trauma, educational aspects, and hearing more about how society works. There are some additions or parts of our identities that we cannot control.

I have a better sense of what played a hand in my own development—how I needed to learn through the development of others as well. No, not being an overly nosy person, but gathering that an individualistic approach will open conversations and, in turn, growth. It's how I learned that some identities can be less linear and more fluid; there can be a sliding scale connected to a box.

This opened a few doors for me, one of them relating to my frustrations as a new collegiate member where decisions were being challenged based on perceptions of a sorority member. Maybe I didn't need the feminine box to exist in my world because it wasn't true to my identity; I just needed a sliding scale that allowed me to move the tab to a comfortable space between masculinity and femininity. No one used a sliding scale when they were searching for potential new members for a sorority.

That is where most people can miss out on experiencing change and success through others: when they neglect to offer them an opportunity to be more than what's written on the walls or on paper. It's seeing something that they might not envision in themselves yet.

Sometimes I think about myself as the nineteen-year-old girl, and how it felt lonely without any options in being fulfilled. I thank her for breaking away from external limits so that I could be open with endless possibilities for my internal growth.

The lesson is that learning to understand yourself is necessary before understanding others; in accepting the diverse nature of life and people, we can not only be better leaders, but more self-aware versions of ourselves.

How do you take time to learn more about yourself, reader; how do you make others feel comfortable being themselves around you? Reflect on your own "ritual" and what values you cherish enough to share with others who may teach you a thing or two. If you want to be a leader in your life, then look no further than how you experience your boxes and all your sliding scales.

Mel Lewis is a proud Charter member of Alpha Omicron Pi who has committed to the Fraternal Movement and works within her passion for student development. As a first-generation college student, she attended Ramapo College of New Jersey for undergrad and achieved her Master of Science in Education at Monmouth University. Mel has advised and worked with fraternity and sorority members from NIC, NPHC, NALFO, MGC, and NPC and has volunteered with her own organization since being initiated into alumna status. Mel transitioned from a campus-based professional to a headquarters staff and became the first Director of Education and Programs for Alpha Chi Rho National Fraternity. She thrives when she is working with students around mental health, growth, development, sexual violence, and inclusivity. She also holds the title for Most Likely to Defend New Jersey!

More information: www.greekuniversity.org/mel

CHAPTER 2

Prioritizing Mental Health during Transition

Greg Vogt

C ollege is a time of excitement, opportunity, and transition for students. With that new experience comes unfamiliarity, uncertainty, and responsibility. Stepping into the unknown poses many challenges. A consistent practice toward mental health and developing strategies to cope with difficulties will be paramount to enact for students, campus leaders, and every fraternity and sorority member. Before we develop an effective outlook, we must understand what mental health is, why it's important, and pinpoint challenges that colleges are facing.

Over the last several years, there has been a positive development that people are beginning to talk more openly about mental health. However, the jargon often gets jumbled when people hear the words *mental health, mental health challenge, mental disorder,* and so on. Being certified in Mental Health First Aid through the National Council for Behavioral Health has provided extensive training and equipped me to understand these different dynamics.

What Mental Health Is

According to NCBH, "*mental health* is a state of well-being in which an individual realizes their own abilities, can cope with normal stressors of life, can work productively and fruitfully, and contributes to their community."[1]

A *mental health challenge,* as defined by NCBH, is "when there is a major change in a person's thinking, feeling, or acting, and the change interferes with the person's ability to live their life, and the interference doesn't go away quickly and lasts longer than typical emotions or reactions would be expected to."

NCBH defines a *mental disorder* as "a diagnosable disorder that affects a person's thinking, emotional state, and behavior, and it disrupts the ability to work, carry out daily activities, and engage in satisfying relationships."

We must be cognizant and empathetic in knowing that those around us may be experiencing a mental health challenge or living with a mental illness. For the purpose of this conversation, we'll be focusing on mental health and its importance to college students. Anything can affect the

---

[1] Definitions are through training by NCBH. For more information, see
   https://www.who.int/mental_health/who_urges_investment/en/

stability or instability of one's mental health: relationships, work, finances, spirituality, diet, hobbies, major life events, goals, distractions, and so on. Reaching optimum mental health takes time, practice, self-discipline, discernment, accountability, and often, professional help.

Why Mental Health Matters

Having suffered from major depressive disorder and anxiety, spending a year in a treatment center, and knowing many people, young and old, who have struggled with mental health, I encourage you to ponder this point. Mental health matters because there is a near guarantee that all of us fall into at least one of these three buckets:

1. We are currently experiencing a mental health challenge or mental disorder ourselves
2. We may experience a challenge at some point in the future
3. We all know at least one person who is currently struggling

We need a simple, yet meaningful approach in de-stigmatizing the conversation on mental health. No matter who you are, where you live, what you stand for, or what your background is, we all know someone who is struggling, if it's not us ourselves. Let's not overcomplicate it; we all have a mind, and the degree of health of that mind can vary due to a variety of reasons. Reminding ourselves that mental health is the health of one's brain, and understanding that we all share that commonality, will position us to be in the same playing field together as allies.

It's important to understand what's taking place at colleges across the country, especially when the picture is pre-conceived going into it. We often hear phrases like, "the best four years of your life," "the greatest time of opportunity," or "the most fun you'll ever have." These statements may or may not be accurate for each person. One thing they do accomplish is setting the bar ultimately high for incoming freshmen. Often what we see next is feelings of failure, insecurity, not meeting expectations, and deep mental health effects.

The Reality of What's Happening on College Campuses

As great as it is to see society gravitate toward a more open dialogue on mental health, there is a stigma that still often exists. This stigma may prevent those who are struggling from speaking up and seeking help. One of the ways to break the stigma and normalize the conversation is to discuss the realities of what's taking place. For the purpose of mental health among the college demographic, we'll take a look at data conducted by Active Minds, the nation's premier nonprofit organization for mental health education and awareness among college students. Below is a brief overview on some of the statistics Active Minds has uncovered regarding the mental health of students in the United States today:

- Suicide is the second leading cause of death among young adults
- 1 in 5 adults have a diagnosable mental illness
- 75% of mental health issues begin by age 24
- 39% of college students experience a significant mental health issue
- 50% of us will experience a mental health condition in our lifetime[2]

As staggering as some of these numbers may be, what's most important to understand is that it is common to struggle. Students are pressed with high academic benchmarks, pressure to fit in socially, financial constraints, increased time spent on social media, and are suffering from loneliness like we've never seen before. These are real challenges and there is no shame or guilt in having a tough time with your mental health. What you're currently going through does not define you and it certainly does not make you less than anyone else. You are not alone in what you're going through, nor in what you're thinking or feeling. However, just like how our feelings, emotions, and mentality matter, being deliberate in how we respond to stressors is equally critical.

Looking back in hindsight, I personally checked several of these statistical boxes above. I struggled with my mental health severely for four years and did not respond in an effective way. But when I found the help that I needed, I learned what it means to prioritize mental health and how to respond to challenges in a meaningful way. My hope is that my story can be a light for you.

---

[2] https://www.activeminds.org/about-mental-health/statistics/

My Mental Health Journey

Growing up in sunny Southern California with a supportive family, friends, and a love for basketball led me to have a hopeful approach for the future. Life was relatively simple and routine during childhood. As I entered high school, there were great expectations of what I thought the experience would be like. Little did I know, high school turned out to be just the opposite of that for me. My basketball career hit a screeching halt and the dreams I had went down with it. My commitment to academics began to wither. I faced social pressures, romantic challenges, and difficulties building true friendships.

What used to be a happy-go-lucky kid suddenly became anxious and insecure. During this time, I was convinced that the only reason my life began heading downward was because of these external challenges I was facing. However, looking back in hindsight, there were some internal voids. I was blaming others for my own wrongdoings, not taking ownership over my mistakes, and making excuses for just about everything. I was unwilling to look for change.

This mentality paired with these external difficulties sent me down a dark road. Those initial feelings turned into a hatred toward life, isolation, loneliness, anxiety, and depression. At the age of sixteen, I was diagnosed with major depressive disorder and subsequently placed on antidepressant medications. It reached the tipping point when I became convinced that suicide seemed like the only option, and attempted to end my life on two different occasions.

Little did I know of what was coming next. I was placed in a residential treatment center for the next twelve months.

I was overwhelmed, fearful, and bitter entering this facility. This transition felt too daunting to get through. The first few months felt like it was low after low. The light at the end of the tunnel often seemed nonexistent. The adjustment to living at a treatment center was steeper than I could have ever expected. No family, no friends, no car, no technological devices, staff monitored 24/7, no access to leaving the facility. The list goes on and on. Who was I to be able to navigate this?

After a couple months, and as I just tried to get by each day, I began to notice some positive realizations. I witnessed that there were many staff members on campus that cared about me. I learned that the other kids had challenges of their own, and was reminded that I wasn't alone. There were resources, therapy, and programs in place for us to get support and stay accountable. Mental health wasn't just a background topic; it was an integral part of day-to-day life. Vulnerability, and truly opening up about our thoughts and feelings was a key focus at this facility as well.

The point is that this treatment center turned out to be the help I needed, even though it wasn't the help I wanted. As I grasped the notion that this was a tremendous opportunity for me to grow, I woke up each day with the mentality to try my best and take baby steps. I listened and trusted the people and professionals around me. I found a community where mental health was a focus and where I didn't feel like an outcast. The twelve-month stay was a roller coaster to say the least, but I eventually completed the treatment program while graduating from high school and returning home with my diploma.

Looking back on this experience, I want to leave you with two things to ponder. The first is that getting help is courageous. For me, help turned out to be in the form of a treatment center. But for you, maybe it's a friend, family member, counseling center, or therapist. The second tip is that this experience showed me that our lives often flow in the direction of our strongest thoughts. When my strongest thoughts in high school were, *I'm a loser; I'm never going to amount to anything; Maybe life isn't worth it,* well, my life was on the brink. But this experience at treatment taught me that fixating our minds on hope and progress, often move our lives in a positive trajectory.

Since the completion of the treatment program, I went on to attend and graduate from the University of Arizona. I joined a fraternity while in school, which was a positive part of my collegiate experience. Three months prior to graduation, my first book, *The Battle Against Yourself,* was published. This provides a deeper look into my story in dealing with mental health challenges, and was written to support students who feel stuck and are struggling to find light at the end of the tunnel in their current circumstances. Now, I get the privilege to speak to students across the country in partnership with Greek University, Active Minds, and the Depression and Bipolar Support Alliance (California).

I say these things for no other reason than that none of these joys in life would be possible if I had never learned to prioritize my mental health. If I continued to place it on the backburner like I did in high school, there's no telling where I'd be today. Through getting professional help, building real relationships, living vulnerably, and getting accountability, the trajectory has been positive.

Solutions and Support

Whether you're a freshman who's been on campus a matter of weeks, a student who's more established, or a campus professional, we all have a role to play in supporting those around us with their mental health, while also keeping it a priority in our own journey. Remember, that mental health matters because we're either going through challenges now, will at some point in the future, or we know someone that is struggling. I'd like to encourage you with solutions and support when it comes to prioritizing mental health during times of transition.

Each mental health challenge, mental illness, or life stressor has its different factors and dynamics. There isn't necessarily a one-size-fits-all approach to resolving the different struggles we face. They often vary from person to person. But as someone who has struggled deeply with my mental health, I'd like to share some solutions and approaches that have helped me gain stability and build a strong foundation to combat the challenges I still face from time to time.

Solution #1: Identify the source of the problem before jumping to solutions.

We as a society are great at trying to find quick fixes to problems. But when we do this, we often misidentify or fail to identify the cause of the problem, and therefore, come to the wrong solution. So, whatever you're going through or feeling, I encourage you to uncover the root of what's causing it before trying to find solutions. If you need help on discovering what that might be, invite a trusted friend, family member, or therapist to help provide an outside perspective.

Solution #2: Practice and live vulnerably.

Vulnerability is one of those buzz words that people either love or despise. Living vulnerably takes effort and practice, but it's been one of the integral parts to my mental health. I've always liked the way Brené Brown sums up vulnerability. She is known as one of the world's top researchers on shame, courage, and vulnerability. Through her research, Brown has uncovered that at the core, people long for three things; joy, connection, and belonging. Since those are the goal, then there must be an avenue to get there. Vulnerability is that avenue. In order to enact vulnerability, Brown states that we must have the willingness to step into conversations that require emotional exposure, risk, and uncertainty—three words that may make most of us cringe, but a requirement nonetheless. Living vulnerably can be the enabler to meaningful connections and a bridge to building positive mental health.

Solution #3: Build authentic relationships and understand that seeking help is courageous.

Piggy-backing off of vulnerability, leaning into those relationships that are full of trust, love, and care should be prioritized. In a society that paints a false narrative that more social media followers mean more happiness, we must combat that by leaning into those interpersonal relationships that act like a two-way street. Cherish those people in your life who constantly pour into you and care for you, and reciprocate the factor for them. And know that when you're in a time that needs a greater sense of urgency beyond your interpersonal network, it is courageous to acknowledge your need, seek support, and proactively ask for help.

Support

If you or someone you know is having a bad day, tough week, or experiencing a mental health challenge that may not be a time of crisis, it's important to show up and support. Know that you don't have to be an expert, but you do have a responsibility to show up and be present. Developing a self-care plan by focusing on what you enjoy can be a good strategy to stabilize the mind when stressed. Leaning into hobbies, people you love, and other priorities can help you stay on the path when those bad days come along.

Conversely, if you or someone you know is in a time of crisis, then the steps for help look very different. A time of crisis can be any point when an individual is in danger; physically, mentally, or emotionally. The key step here would be to point that person toward professional help immediately. In a potential life-threatening instance, 9-1-1 should be called. Otherwise, calling the National Suicide Prevention Lifeline at (800) 273-8255, texting HOME to the Crisis Text Line at 741741, or visiting a psychologist or psychiatrist could serve as viable options. These are general suggestions, and it should be noted that each situation requires different measures.

Final Thoughts

My hope is that wherever you're at in life—whether you've dealt with mental health challenges or not—that we all walk away with a better understanding of what mental health is, how it's affecting college students, and what we can do to support those around us. If it wasn't for the help and support I received, life would look a lot different today. Each day presents new challenges, and our mental health can waver as the stages of life shift. When we work to understand our challenges, live vulnerably, understand the courage in seeking help, and support one another in prioritizing mental health, then I believe we'll be positioned to thrive in times of transition, during college, and for the years proceeding.

Greg Vogt is a Professional Mental Health Speaker with Greek University. He also speaks in partnership with Active Minds, the nation's premier nonprofit organization for mental health among young adults. Greg serves as a Board Member for the Depression & Bipolar Support Alliance (California). His efforts in serving the mental health community blossomed after publishing his first book in 2017, *The Battle Against Yourself.* This depicts his personal battles with mental health challenges—from anxiety, depression, and suicidal ideation, to attending a residential treatment center for a year-long program, leading to recovery.

Greg holds a Bachelor's Degree in Marketing and Entrepreneurship from the University of Arizona. During his time as a student, he joined Kappa Alpha Order as a Re-Founding Father. Greg also has four years of corporate experience working for a Fortune 50 company. Most importantly, Greg is a husband, son, brother, and friend.

He enjoys spending time with loved ones, traveling to new places, trying different foods, playing sports, writing poetry, and serving in children's ministry at the local church.

More information: www.greekuniversity.org/greg

CHAPTER 3

Understanding Majority Privilege

Robert Wilson

Some time ago, I was hired to conduct an on-line workshop on inclusion and diversity for a prominent university. A few weeks prior to the workshop, the event team was on a Zoom call prepping for the session, when one of the organizers asked if I would be speaking about privilege. I explained that privilege is one of the so-called "inclusion derailers" I focus on during the workshop and that we would be doing an activity to help students and staff understand the nature of privilege.

The man immediately scoffed as his face sunk. He told me he was disappointed I would be talking about privilege because he did not believe privilege was a real thing. He described his lower socioeconomic upbringing and he shared his personal story of hardship along his journey to his current position at the university. He was concerned that conversations about privilege alienate many whites and men, and he felt the concept provided an excuse for women and students of color when they encountered the challenges that life eventually confronts all of us with. I listened intently without interrupting. When he was finished, I paused for a moment and began to explain privilege in the same terms that I have used to explain the concept to audiences all over the world.

By nature of you reading this book, you have privilege. If you are a student or a staff member or administrator at a college or university, you have privilege. If you have participated in a Zoom call or attended a live webinar or in-person speech on any number of topics affecting Greek or student life, you have privilege. Society at large tends to focus on two types of privilege. Male privilege and white privilege. Male privilege and white privilege are real living and breathing factors that can negatively impact the outcomes of those who lack these two types of privilege. It is not my intention to minimize them. However, they don't tell the entire story and there are many other types of privilege. There is straight privilege and able-bodied or neurological privilege or even socioeconomic privilege, which my colleague called out during that Zoom call. For this reason, I prefer to use the term *"majority privilege."* In fact, whenever you have a minority group and a majority group in any setting, the same types of instinctive human behavior begin to bear themselves out. I will prove this to you using a very simple activity.

Which hand is your dominant hand? Are you left-handed or right-handed or ambidextrous? Most of the people reading this chapter are right-handed. In fact, statistically, 90 percent of humans are right-handed. Now think for a moment about your experience as a right-handed person or a left-handed person in our society. If you are right-handed, what types of challenges or obstacles have you faced? Perhaps you have struggled trying to drive an automobile in a right-hand drive country like England or Australia? Or maybe you recall constantly bumping the left-handed person you recently sat next to at dinner. Or worse, perhaps your burgeoning major league baseball career was stunted due to your inability to drive a fastball thrown by a left-handed pitcher. Beyond these mostly minor nuisances, what tangible challenges or obstacles have you truly faced as a result of your being right-hand dominant?

Now consider the experiences of our left-handed neighbors, coworkers, classmates, relatives, children, or spouse. What challenges have they faced? How easy has it been for them to do fairly mundane tasks, like finding a comfortable desk in class. How about writing on a white board and erasing what you just wrote with your sleeves. How about locating sports equipment or paying the same price for the equipment a right-handed person pays when they finally find it. What about driving an automobile? Who are cars laid out for? Where is the shifter? How about the controls? How about something as simple as shaking hands? How easy or natural is it to shake hands with your off hand? If you are the parent of a left-handed child, how easy is it to teach them simple tasks like tying a tie or even their shoelaces? What about learning to play an instrument from a right-handed person? And lastly, how many pairs of left-handed scissors were there in first or second grade? The world is designed by and for the majority, right-handers. And if you are right-handed, you rarely have to consider the experiences of left-handed people.

You have the luxury of ambivalence toward the challenges of the minority group. That is what majority privilege is. And majority privilege is literally everywhere, impacting the experiences we have day-to-day in our communities, workplaces, classrooms, and even our homes. Let's dissect majority privilege further.

How do we see ourselves based on our majority or minority group status? Oftentimes, those in the majority see themselves as individuals and minorities as members of a homogeneous group. Have you ever had a discussion about race in a class and the focus of the conversation turned to the one black person in the classroom? The "minority" was expected to educate the majority about race as if their experience was representative of everyone within their racial group. If you are white, have you ever been asked to explain the perspectives of white people as a group? If you have, did you respond with disdain at the mere suggestion that you could speak for all white people? If you relate to a majority identity group, you may not even perceive yourself as part of a group. However, you tend to perceive the minority as one homogenous group which is unfair to the individuals who make up that group. The majority group has to be aware and avoid treating the outgroup or minority group as homogenous.

There is a lesson in majority privilege for the minority as well. Although we know that there are more evil people left in the world than any of us would care to admit, in many cases in our day-to-day lives, people in the majority group are just unaware. Sometimes when you are in a minority group it's easy to believe that every slight or microaggression is due to your minority status. Most of the time, that is not the case. The majority group is simply clueless.

Years ago I worked as a young engineer in a manufacturing plant. I was one of few black engineers in the plant. I recall the difficulty fitting in during lunch conversations or casual conversations with white engineers or white supervisors around the plant. There were even comments made about things going on in society or everyday life that seemed tone deaf to my experience as a young black man. My perception some days was that I was in a sea of racists all working toward one goal: to ensure my failure. This persisted during the early part of my engineering career. The problem was the duality of the people I worked with. They were equally capable of making an insensitive racial remark as they were to stay late helping me work through an engineering issue I was struggling with. I never understood this dynamic until majority privilege was explained to me. And it was very liberating for me to realize that most of my coworkers, many of whom I liked and credit with my early success, were probably not racists or trying to ensure my failure. They were just clueless. They had lived their life in the majority, never having to walk a day in my shoes. And so they were clueless as to the challenges and obstacles that existed for people who looked like me and came from where I came from. Therein lies one of the key lessons of majority privilege for those in the minority. Today, in the second decade of the twenty-first century, there is likely not a meeting of the minds each morning to plan how to ruin the lives of left-handers. The righties are just clueless.

One of the more interesting nuances of majority privilege is how the majority tends to react when confronted with their privilege. It is not so different from how my colleague reacted on that Zoom call. Men often deny that their male status has had anything to do with their success in a mostly male work or classroom environment. People born into wealth believe their hard work was the predominant driver for their life achievements. Straight people are loathe to speak about LGTBQ issues, often hiding behind the excuse that "sexual orientation is no one's business" just before digressing into conversations about their hetero-led family's weekend activities. Able-bodied people take it personal when a wheel-chaired friend admonishes them for constantly holding the door. And many of us become very uncomfortable around relatives and friends who have learning, mental health, or other neurological challenges.

Take the example of the eight-year-old left-handed child who one day grows impatient with the lack of left-handed scissors in the classroom. If you are right-handed and have ever tried to cut with left-handed scissors, you know why. It physically hurts to use them. So this child decides to say something to their teacher about the lack of left-handed scissors. How does the likely right-handed teacher, consumed with mischievous children and the other legitimate pressures of teaching, likely react? "Share the left-handed pair!" she might exclaim. Or "We don't have the budget for more scissors. Use what you have." Or perhaps, "Is it really that difficult?" The majority group hates to be called out for their lack of empathy toward the challenges of the minority group. Their reaction is often loaded with defensiveness, denial, annoyance, or even anger. Why is this? What is actually happening?

In the 1960s, the Gallup organization conducted a series of polls of white Americans all over the country on their attitudes regarding the Civil Rights Movement. In one of the questions, whites were asked if they thought the work of civil rights leaders like Dr. King, "sit-ins at lunch counters, freedom buses, and other demonstrations by Negroes will hurt or help the Negroes' chances of being integrated in the South?" Fifty-seven percent of whites replied that the movement was hurting their chances. In another study, 60 percent of whites disapproved of the March on Washington! Even with the difficult racial discourse we face today, we'd still expect overwhelming white approval of the heroic work civil rights leaders and activists, white and black, undertook during the 1950s and 1960s to help create a "more perfect union."

So why this reaction during the actual time the minority group was trying to change the power dynamic? The majority group does not like to have their majority status challenged. When the world you live, work, or study in has been set up by people like you, for people like you, any slight change in the power dynamic, feels like a loss, a major challenge to your majority status. Humans do not like change, and most of all, the majority does not like to have their grip on the institutions they control put at risk.

So what do we do with our newfound knowledge of how privilege works? All of us at one point or another, find ourselves either beneficiaries or sufferers at the hand of majority privilege. Understanding the instincts at play when our brains are confronted with majority privilege does not absolve us of responsibility to mitigate its effects on our relationships and communities. A final look back in history provides us a roadmap to how best to navigate majority privilege.

In 1920, after decades of activism in favor of women's suffrage, the United States, ratified the 19th Amendment, which gave women the right to vote. Pioneering women like Sojourner Truth, Elizabeth Stanton, Mary Church Terrell, and Susan B. Anthony worked tirelessly, fighting for the rights of women. No matter how hard they fought, it was white men who had to be incentivized and convinced that women's suffrage was right for the country.

The 1960s were a tumultuous time, during which the most sweeping civil rights legislation since the Reconstruction period was passed, laws that shape the American experience today and beyond. The struggle and perseverance and ultimately sacrifice of civil rights patriots like Dr. Martin Luther King Jr., Dianne Nash, Malcolm X, Rosa Parks, Andrew Young, and John Lewis were responsible for holding America accountable to the democracy we call the greatest in the world. But ultimately it was whites across the country who joined them and responded to the injustice of segregation and Jim Crow that led to the passing of the Civil Rights Act of 1964 and other landmark legislation of the Lyndon Johnson presidency.

The advances in societal attitudes toward LGBTQ rights from 2000–2015 represented one of the greatest civil rights opinion shifts in US history. This shift was not by accident, the result of Marriage Equality advocates like those who risk their careers, families, and their lives daily so that they could have the same equal protection under the law that straight couples were afforded. Their sacrifice was great but it was their work to compel straight people to their position and their cause that led to the Supreme Court's landmark decision legalizing gay marriage in 2014.

Privilege has to be extended from those who have it to those who need more of it. It is the responsibility of those in the majority to extend their privilege to those among us who, often simply because of circumstances of birth, lack the privilege they need to compete on an even playing field. It is not enough for the majority to focus on what they don't do, rather they must move off the sideline, onto the field of battle and direct their privilege for the benefit of our institutions, our workplaces, our families, and our relationships. That is the true lesson of majority privilege.

Robert Lawrence Wilson is a speaker, facilitator, and writer with expertise in diversity and inclusion, multicultural outreach marketing and leadership development. Cofounder of the Culture Shift Team, he leads their diversity strategy development and training across all platforms and markets from higher education and non-profit to corporate.

Robert began his journey in diversity and inclusion as an undergraduate at the University of Michigan, where he served as a residence hall diversity peer advisor. He has served in executive roles at Nissan North America, including as the company's first Director of Diversity and Inclusion and as Director of Customer Experience. He developed and led Nissan's diversity practice and multicultural market strategy for the Americas.

Robert serves on the leadership boards of several nonprofit organizations promoting greater access to quality education for the nation's most at-risk student population. He is also cofounder of the Tennessee Diversity Consortium. Robert holds a bachelor's degree in mechanical engineering from the University of Michigan and a master's degree in business administration from Duke University.

More information: www.greekuniversity.org/robert

CHAPTER 4

Don't Haze the Newcomers, Mentor Them

Hank Nuwer

Most successful people I know have given credit for that success to a mentor. The few who didn't have a mentor say the lack of one delayed or detoured their careers. Today, young men and women seek inspiration from seasoned pros in business, athletics, the arts, law, medicine, and student affairs.

Suffice to say that every fraternal chapter should make sure that those assigned to be big brothers or big sisters actually are mentoring in caring, productive ways. Those few who haze instead of mentor do a double disservice to the newcomers under them.

They breed mistrust. They create a fraternal environment with relentless emphasis on shame and foolish risk-taking that is blatantly stultifying for the new members of fraternal families.

What Is a Mentor?

The classic book *Seasons of a Man's Life* by Yale psychologist Daniel J. Levinson calls mentoring "one of the most complex and developmentally important [relationships]" of early adulthood.[3]

Mentors go way back in time. It's no stretch to picture a hairy caveman showing a younger, fuzz-faced comrade the proper way to mix dyes and paint bison on cave walls. That way, even if a pterodactyl whisked away the older artist for a one-course lunch, the surviving artist knew how to preserve the tried-and-true skills, but maybe added a few retro futurism touches to spiffy up those walls.

The term "mentor" was inspired by the poet Homer's character named (no surprise!) Mentor. The warrior Odysseus charged Mentor with protecting his household and schooling his son Telemachus during his wandering years of the Trojan Wars.

Significantly, to put it bluntly, Mentor was a poor mentor. He failed to keep out the riff-raff suitors that bullied and hazed young Telemachus and harassed faithful Penelope.

---

[3] Daniel J. Levinson, *Seasons of a Man's Life* (New York: Random House, 1978), 97.

But his name has become synonymous with trusted advisors who counsel and teach, the lesson being that a poor mentor like the Greek Mentor is worse than no mentor at all. A cautionary example of the latter occurs in the classic movie *Wall Street* when the avaricious Gordon Gekko (Michael Douglas) uses and abuses Bud Fox (Charlie Sheen).

The best fraternal mentor-mentee relationships are those in which an experienced master embraces the duties of sponsoring a novice and boosting him or her up the career ladder. Interestingly, your direct supervisor is rarely or never your mentor, because the supervisory role prohibits him or her from being a mentor in the strictest sense. The supervisor, unlike the mentor, is there to show you the ropes, not throw you a lifeline such as a promotion.

Don't Treat a Newcomer as a "Rookie"

During my half-century as a reporter, I've frequently written about win-win mentoring examples.

One of those involved a newcomer and an old pro in the thrilling, oft-dangerous field of lumberjack sports.

Mike Sullivan, a onetime major league baseball hopeful whose career ended due to an injury to his throwing arm, credits an old pro and sometimes log-bucking partner named Jim Colbert for propelling him to twenty all-around lumberjack wins in his first three years as a competitor.

Colbert, many years Mike's senior, not only taught Sullivan the art of sawing and chopping, he also lent him his expensive equipment until Mike could save enough to purchase his own costly saws, axes, and other gear.

In one of my numerous interviews with Sullivan who I shadowed for several national magazines, he referred to Colbert as one of the most unselfish persons he's ever met. "When I win, he's proud," Sullivan said. "And if anybody beats me, I want it to be him."

It is very common, no matter the field, for mentors and mentees to work shoulder to shoulder. Thus, it occurred one year that I covered Sullivan and Colbert teaming up at a Lumberjack World Championship in Hayward, Wisconsin. The two-man team set a new world record in the two-man crosscut sawing event.

Today, Sullivan is the undisputed Paul Bunyan of lumberjack sports and Colbert is retired. And that is the indisputable reality of mentor-mentee relationships. One day the newcomer surpasses the teacher who bows out.

So, it's no surprise that Sullivan to this day is considered a mentor by several talented new axe-and-saw challengers. And the cheerleader Colbert now shouts encouragement to Mike from the comfort of his living room couch.

Disappoint a Mentor at Your Own Risk

When I was in elementary and high school, about the only thing keeping my self-esteem alive was baseball. I served as captain of Little League, Babe Ruth, and American Legion teams.

Unquestionably I owed any and all successes to my first coach, Steve Bania, a one-time minor leaguer for Spokane who saw promise in me. Long after the other players left the field for the town swimming pool, Steve hit me hundreds of grounders at first and pitched batting practice until his arm ached. Winters, I sat on Steve's home davenport to listen to his baseball tips and tales, while his wife, Berniece, served us cookies and Kool-Aid.

Steve was a one-of-a-kind mentor who gave praise only when deserved and who brooked no disrespect to the game of baseball he so loved. Thus, it happened at age eleven, when a big, nasty opponent drove his spikes into my Keds as I took a throw at first, I dropped him with one punch as my war veteran dad had taught me during self-defense lessons.

Steve pulled me from the game and sent me home in disgrace with parting words I never forgot—even when I later sometimes ignored his wisdom—a risk all mentors understand. "You let him take you down to his level."

I never again fought on the diamond, and Steve the next game restored my captaincy. I singled with my Nellie Fox bottle bat in my first at-bat back, and he gave me the okay sign with finger and thumb.

No one was more thrilled than Steve when years later on assignments for magazines, I played first base in spring training for two Montreal Expos minor league teams and later played for the Indianapolis Clowns, the Negro League team that gave Hammering Hank Aaron his start. I didn't start for either, but I played hard.

Coach and I corresponded right up to the day he passed too young from early-onset diabetes. If now and forever I can perform at Steve Bania's "level," I'll never disappoint my baseball mentor watching from heaven again.

The point I wanted to make is that fraternities and sororities provide members an invaluable opportunity for mentoring. Whether varsity teams or intermural club sports, opportunities in Greek groups are boundless for opportunities to bond veteran and younger players. To this day I correspond regularly with members of Buffalo State's baseball team with whom I played, as well as with a couple dozen fraternity brothers with whom I played in intermural track, flag football, softball, and basketball.

If team sports aren't your cup of tea, a shared love for good health and fitness is how many mentors and potential protégés connect. Many neophytes find a mentor sweating bullets and pounds off at the school or company fitness center. "Fitness is a great equalizer," according to Michael G. Zey, PhD, author of *The Mentor Connection*.

Greek Faculty and Active Alumni

One of the best traditions my own fraternity at Buffalo State College sponsored was the opportunity to interact with the chapter's honorary faculty and engaged alums. This was done collectively once a year at a spaghetti and salad feast, as well as an informal hayride and barn dance each fall.

One of the faculty alums was a well-published and adventurous white-haired professor in his fifties who chatted with me in his office about his own experiences as a chapter member at the University of Vermont. As a result, I signed up for his classes, forever altering my life for the better.

It turned out that he had traveled to Cuba to interview Ernest Hemingway and Vermont to chat with Robert Frost in his smoky cabin. "Don't teach your students a lesson, show them a lesson," the old poet and teacher advised my new mentor Fraser Drew. And Drew's classes electrified not only me, a confirmed jock, but others. So much so that Drew became the first winner of the State University of New York Distinguished Teaching Professor award.

My faculty brother's influence lasted beyond my graduation—a graduation incidentally in which I received the English Department's Contemporary Literature award.

One day I shyly brought him a batch of unpublished poems and short stories to critique. He told me, realistically, that I should put away my pipe dream of playing major league baseball and to pursue a career as a journalist and writer. More importantly, he showed me the difference between a good line in my stories and the ones needing reworking.

Unknown to me at the time, a good mentor softens criticism of a mentee's work with the soothing balm of praise. What's also clear is that every good mentor possesses the trait of empathy. This is another reason that mentors do not haze their mentees or expect predatory sexual favors from them. Hazing, by its nature, creates stress in young males and females. A good mentor tries hard to keep the relationship stress-free.

It's crucial to know that not all mentors have your best interests at heart. Learn to spot the leeches before they drain your ideas and creativity. In some fields, such as scholarly research or the software industry, so-called "mentors" have taken younger associates under their wings and then taken undeserved credit in publications.

The relationship with my mentor ended when he died at age 100, but not before we published a book collection of our literary letters to one another written during four decades of friendship. He also wrote convincing letters of reference that earned me college teaching jobs and convinced my alma mater to offer me an honorary doctorate. I spoke at Buffalo State commencement in 2006. The other commencement speaker was Hillary Clinton, former U.S. Secretary of State. My talk was dedicated to one person. I'm sure you know his identity.

And to top it off, I named my younger son Drew.

What the Experts Say about Mentoring

One of my favorite jobs was working as a contributing writer to *Men's Fitness*. One of the many articles I wrote for the magazine was a collection of interviews with nationally known experts on mentoring.

My favorite interviewee was therapist Anthony P. (Tony) Jurich, a professor at Kansas State University, who unfortunately drowned while on vacation, Professor Jurich told me that everyone needs someone to provide guidance, support, and advice, particularly at the beginning of a career or an important life event such as pledging.

"A mentor is not only important; having one is almost a necessity," Jurich said. He himself cited scholar Carlfred Broderick, PhD, as the mentor who changed his own life. Broderick taught him to be enthused about enabling patients who sought therapy. He described Broderick as the ideal mentor who seemed "enthused" about helping him.

Zey cautioned that mentees must guard against becoming overly dependent. Mentors die, get transferred, leave for a new field. It's important that you get to know and work with a lot of people. He recommended that those seeking mentors put themselves in a position to contribute—even in a minor way—to the organization's major projects. He suggested that you make contact with people in power. Expose yourself to people in higher management by working on "A" projects, not "B" projects. Don't get into the rut of repeatedly supporting inconsequential projects.[4]

Some Words of Caution

Thank your stars again if your national fraternity or other organization offers a structured mentor program. Otherwise, finding the right mentor can seem as difficult as landing a significant other.

---

[4] Michel G. Zey, *The Mentor Connection: Strategic Alliances in Corporate Life* (New Brunswick, NJ: Transaction Publishers, 2002), 177.

Coming on too strong can turn off or even frighten a potential mentor. In that case, expect to be shown the door, not the light.

"The mentor should see you as an up-and-coming star," Zey cautioned me in an interview for *Men's Fitness* magazine. "You can't be cold-blooded. What you have to be is confident. You want to get people's attention, but that won't happen if you're not confident."

What's in It for the Mentor?

If you already possess a mentor, thank the lucky Dogstar that sent this gifted person your way.

If you do not, whether you are a new student affairs professional or a graduate student—or whatever—be on the lookout for someone successful who inspires you, as well as someone unselfish who rejoices in your successes as if they were his or her own.

Jurich warned me that some mentors, unfortunately, give way to their baser instincts when the mentee surpasses the mentor. He urged great communication at the outset of the relationship to dispel that eventuality. "The mentor should say, 'I expect you to eclipse me. If you don't, that's okay; if you do, that's okay, too.' That's got to be set up at the very beginning and be very explicit."

So, what is in it for the mentor? "The mentor gets to share his or her career peak," Jurich said. "He'll have the satisfaction of knowing his experience and ability will live on when he's moved on."

Final Thoughts

The one place I failed to find a mentor was a two-year stretch at a Catholic seminary in Buffalo, New York.

Not only did I rail against the priest-professors who taught by rote memory alone as if this were still the Middle Ages, but I found myself without a single supporter when the rector caught me and a classmate's sister exchanging kisses in a classroom on Family Visitation Day.

Growing up, I loved the priests played by Bing Crosby in *Going My Way* and Spencer Tracy in *Boys Town*. I grew disillusioned fast finding none like them at my seminary.

Yes, how different things might be today had I found a priestly mentor. Who knows, by now I might have become the first USA Pope.

Hank Nuwer is the author of *Hazing: Destroying Young Lives, Wrongs of Passage, High School Hazing*, and *The Hazing Reader*. His blog, Hazing Prevention, is part of his website, HankNuwer.com and he now keeps a record of hazing deaths at schools since the first death in 1838. He is an emeritus professor at Franklin College and a full-time author. The ABC-CLIO publishing company contacted Hank to write Hazing in American Culture scheduled for 2022.

This includes the troubling problem of sexual hazing in athletics, on-the-job hazing in professions such as police work and nursing, as well as far more historical research on how hazing infiltrated American academia. He commutes from Indiana to a home in Warsaw and a writing cabin in the woods of Poland where he lives with his wife, Gosia Nuwer. They also have 20 acres in the Alaska bush. His most treasured awards include HazingPrevention.org's Hank

Nuwer Anti-Hazing Award, an honorary State University of New York honorary doctorate, and election to Ball State University Journalism Hall of Fame.

More information: www.greekuniversity.org/hank

CHAPTER 5

UNFROZEN™:
Sexual Assault Prevention, Bystander Intervention Strategy, and the Power of Empathy

Jamie Devin Wilson

*Trigger Warning:

For this chapter, names have been altered for the privacy and safety of all involved.

Please note there are campus and community resources in your area for victims of sexual assault.

I am a survivor of sexual violence, and this is my story.

Twelve years after my assault, 378,432,000 seconds, I finally felt *unfrozen*.

To start, I am a sorority woman who believes in the power of students ending sexual violence on their campuses through bystander intervention strategy, understanding their resources, and being empathetic in the face of disclosure. I was an average student and heavily involved in all aspects of fraternity and sorority life in college. Please stop right there if you think that this story will be bashing fraternity and sorority life, because it is not. It is understanding the power of sharing stories and information to create change. It has made me who I am, changed me, challenged me, and influenced me. I think that being a part of sisterhood has always been the largest influence in my life. Some choose to experience their four years or so and move on. But like Peter Parker's guiding principle, "with great power comes great responsibility," I believe there is a responsibility upon all of us to create a culture of consent on our campuses and educate on empathy. More importantly, in the face of members disclosing their stories, you can help someone feel supported, cared for, and heard. You have the power and resources to know how to respond with empathy and compassion. I want to share my story, so someone else's story can be heard too.

Let me preface the rest of this story that the details of this night only became unlocked in my brain after twelve years of suppression and traumatic response. This is my story of survival, and it was not my fault that this happened to me. No story is the same, and every story is important to tell. One of the most incredible opportunities I have been given is to tell my story to uplift and ignite others' fire to tell their stories. To bring some control and power to survivors' voices and their experiences. This is my experience.

According to RAINN (Rape, Abuse & Incest National Network), 54% of all college-aged students who experienced sexual violence were between 18 and 30 . . . 54%.[5] Let that sink in. More than half of all sexual violence victims are under the age of 30 years old. Think about that. Pause for a minute. Whether you are reading this as a college student, higher education administrator, or someone that has college-aged children, think . . . That fact pulls me back into the same icy cold, numb state as I was once living in for twelve years following my assault.

So let me take you back to my freshman year. Around November 2006, I went to a Fraternity and Life social event. "Buy You a Drank" by T-Pain blasting on the stereos.

People are dancing and drinking. I probably had 1–1.5 full cups of jungle juice that night, and I felt good but not out of control. I remembered the night very well and had a great time. That event was run like a tight ship. We had sober drivers, sober monitors, risk management procedures, and everything was done without any apps, phones, or technology. I felt safe. My sisters knew where I was and when I wanted to leave. I could get into a car and realize I would be safely driven back to my residence hall. That night I got into a car to go back to campus with my best friend at the time and sorority sister, June. We got dropped off at her residence hall because we would hang out a little longer before we called it a night. When we got back to campus, we were hungry. I mean, you know, that night time we were ready for a fourth meal kind of hungry. We ordered a calzone from a prominent place on the top of the University campus and ordered it

---

[5] https://rainn.org/statistics/victims-sexual-violence

to be delivered. We hung out outside for about forty-five minutes when both of us realized it was taking forever.

As we waited, my sorority sister June and I decided that we did not need the calzone as we grew impatient. She asked if I remembered meeting this bouncer guy at the bar named Nathan. She must have been texting him, and he picked us up from the Freshman residence hall area. I honestly went with her because we always have fun together. She seemed interested in Nathan, and I did not want her to go alone. College Jamie was still up for a good time and was happy to join her; again, good friends and sisters don't let other friends go alone.

I wish we waited for the calzone.

I got into a white truck. I remember the vehicle vividly. June sat in the front seat, and I sat in the back. We arrived at a small white house off-campus very close to the food emporium. I remember being a little tipsy but almost sober, and we walked into the living room upon entry. To my left was a large flat-screen TV with a sports game playing on it. Directly in front was a kitchen. My memory only really remembers a hallway and at the end of the hallway a room. June and I were quickly introduced to a reasonably good looking large, tall man I had never met before.

I quickly met some roommate in the kitchen, and Nathan, the guy who picked us up in the white truck talking to June, was there. The whole exchange seemed very quick, and before I knew it, June and Nathan went to that back room. They closed the door, and I just assumed they were hanging out. I sat down on the couch next to the guy I just met. Don introduced himself. I remember feeling small next to him. Since I am a friendly person, I got to know him a bit. We connected, and I was physically attracted to him. He kissed me. I did not mind kissing him. That's all I wanted to do. I remember thinking to myself that I wouldn't mind meeting someone new. I did not feel in control anymore. Very fast, I was being held down with his thick hands. I felt extreme weight and pressure on my thighs and body. He moved me on top of him. I could not remember thinking anything but a blank void. I was nervous, and the only thing I could think of was making sure he used a condom. From there, it got violent. I thought to myself and said out loud, "Where is June?" He ignored my requests.

I felt *frozen*.

When Don wanted to change positions, he called me obscene names and belittled my integrity and body. I remember him calling me names, asking me if I liked it, and then hit me. I remember looking for my little silver flip phone. I remember being frozen. I went along with all of it because I was in total shock. Trauma. Numbness. I couldn't move. He moved me. He abused me. This was not something I wanted. For a very long time, I could not understand why I did not try and leave, fight, or scream. During the assault, Nathan, the acquaintance in the back room with June, came out two times. Once, he high fived Don during the act as I actively asked for June. I am sure my face was less than enthused. The second time he walked out and went into the kitchen and then went back into the room and closed the door. The door shutting behind him felt like the icicles freezing me more and more into submission, into trauma.

Let's do some education quickly here. Consent is not something that can ever be given while intoxicated. Again, consent is not something you can provide while drunk or under the influence of substances. Consent is also fluid. Permission can be given and taken away despite any horrible depictions of sexual encounters in the movies or on television. It is fluid, like choosing hoops instead of stud earrings halfway through the night out. It is deciding how many holes you would like to put those earrings in.

The night I was assaulted, I only wanted to think about trying on the earrings and did not wish to put on any earrings at all. I only consented to kiss. I never consented to anything else.

To end sexual violence on college campuses worldwide, we need to educate and create a culture of consent. We need to remove all awkwardness from the topic and only engage in sexual activities when given enthusiastic consent. We also not only need to educate on bystander intervention strategy but practice it.

I have no idea why and will never know why Nathan did not intervene. I am not going to use this space to speculate if it was planned or random. But if you are a Nathan, please use a basic intervention strategy if you are safe.

Here is my strategy for active bystander intervention. When intervening, the essential thing is that you, as the active bystander, are safe to do so. These are not all mutually exclusive and then do not need to be in any order. If you are unable to do one or more than one, do what you can. The strategy is called UNFROZEN™, this is a straightforward method to help someone who needs it.

U- *Under no circumstance intervene unless you are safe to do so!*

Example from my assault: Many people always ask, if June knew now I was being assaulted, would she have done something. I know deep down that she most likely would have or would have wanted to. That depends on her personal safety. I was violently abused, so I am not sure that it would have been safe to intervene in all these ways, but I am sure she would have chosen a few ways to help.

N- *Nonstop confrontation by being direct, clear, and concise*

Example from my assault: Nathan could have used his power and authority as Don's roommate to say, "Hey buddy, looks like Jamie is feeling uncomfortable." He could then have gotten June and called 911 or asked me what I wanted to do next.

F- *Figure out a way to distract or de-escalate the situation*

Example from my assault: Nathan could have seen what was going on and then could have made noise and acted oddly to draw attention to him.

R- *Remember your resources and delegate to a third-party (911 or your campus hotline)*

Example from my assault: Nathan could have gotten June and asked her to call 911 while he distracted Don from knowing what they were doing.

O- *Orient and organize yourself. Document and take notes on your phone of what you see and document details like addresses, names, etc.*

Z- *Zip up the situation by delaying through checking in with the person being harassed or starting to collect things to leave the situation*

Example from my assault: Nathan could have checked in with me, had June check in with me, could have made sure I was okay and safe.

E- *Engage with empathy*

Example from my assault: Nathan being the only bystander during the assault that knew what was happening, could have engaged with kindness, care, and careful attention to the situation.

N- *No matter what, believe the survivor*

Example from my assault: If the survivor shares that they think they were assaulted, believe them. Period. Do not ask any questions, actively listen.

Talking about believing the survivor, let's get back to that night.

After Don finished, which seemed like hours of violence upon me, it was probably only minutes. I quickly tried to find my silver flip phone. I remember Don asking if I was okay. I did not answer. I just asked to get some air. I remember not being able to move from that couch. A heavy, overwhelming gloom pushed down on me. I couldn't move. I asked where Nathan and June were. I stated I was ready to leave. I felt I was at a standstill. I felt unmovable. I felt heavy. I felt numb. Science tells us that this freeze response in trauma actually happens before fight or flight. Those of us that describe our stories of trauma as feeling frozen the entire time and even after is something called tonic immobility. This happens often in traumatic events such as sexual violence and military trauma.

Shortly after I asked for my phone, June exited the room and entered the living area I was in. Nathan followed her. They looked happy and calm. They didn't seem awkward, and they didn't seem to know what had happened to me. I quickly asked to be driven home.

We got into the white truck. I again sat in the back seat, feeling heavy and frozen in time. You know when you are in the back seat of a car, and you can see the person sitting in front, looking at your facial reactions through the rearview mirror? How you say something and intentionally look for their response. Well, June and Nathan asked how my night was, and I remember pausing and saying as tears formed in my eyes, "I was just raped."

The reaction of Nathan was immediate, "Oh, are you sure? I am sure you probably wanted it." I remember June's eyes; she was shocked and did not respond in the car that night.

That was probably the moment I went into a deep freeze for the next twelve years. The risk manager of my sorority brought me to Health and Wellness on my campus a few days later when she saw the 17-inch black and purple bruise along my thigh, and June came with me to the Women's Center to help me figure out next steps. In my college years, we were never taught what to do when a sister discloses, and I feel now, after many years, those that I did tell, they did what they could. I know better now, and I want to empower and educate those in any uncomfortable situation and those to whom the act is disclosed to, how to interact and react. The answer is and always will be with empathy.

I went to the hospital a couple of days later and got a sexual assault forensic exam, I spoke with the University Conduct Office, I went to a few sessions with someone from the Women's Center, but overall I felt like no matter what, I did not want to continue to retell my story—I wanted this all to go away. I desperately wanted to go home for winter break and forget about what happened. I never filed a police report because I just wanted to finish school and not have anything else to worry about. As I started to push down my feelings on what happened, I noticed I had told a minimal amount of people throughout college. I most likely would have never told another soul than that handful those first few weeks after it happened due to necessity. Junior year, I finally started to thaw out a bit. This was when I met my now-husband.

I told my husband within one week of meeting him my junior year of college. His reaction, "I am so sorry you went through that; how can I help?"

While my junior year was many years ago, that moment of pure empathy, active listening, and someone who believed me wholeheartedly was the moment I started to feel unfrozen. I was far from my road to recovery, though. Even though my husband is a fantastic partner and supporter; it took me about another nine years to feel unfrozen. It was realizing that in the field of work that I am in, to be my best self, I needed therapy to stop the nightmares and panic attacks. For me, it was eye movement desensitization and reprocessing psychotherapy (EMDR). Although challenging and uncomfortable, I realized that revisiting the trauma was the only way for me to know that none of this was my fault. I learned that I could live and be successful even if I hold this trauma with me and understand that trauma lives in the body. I learned that teaching students and people about how to know their resources and how to respond with empathy in the face of disclosure is important. It took twelve whole years to tell my story as a survivor and not a statistic. It took me twelve years to know how to cope with my trauma. It took me twelve years to learn how to help myself and work on myself holistically actively. It took twelve whole years to feel *UNFROZEN.*

Jamie Devin Wilson is on a mission to end sexual violence, educate others in active bystander intervention, and uplift the fraternity and sorority life experience. She cares deeply for the development and growth of not just college students but young professionals in the field of higher education.

She is a wife, sister, sorority woman, survivor of sexual violence, and student affairs professional in higher education. She enjoys coffee, yoga, REALLY long walks, and watching old episodes of *Gossip Girl* and *Greek*. Did we mention she is a sorority woman?!

Fraternity and sorority is woven through her blood, sweat, and tears. Jamie has been working with college students for over ten years in a variety of roles including working for an inter/national sorority, on college campuses, and through facilitating and speaking.

Jamie graduated with a bachelor's degree in journalism, and a minor in leadership from the University of Rhode Island. After graduating she spent some time working in sales and for a social media marketing company. Shortly after, she worked for her inter/national organization in a variety of roles as a consultant, membership manager, and house director. After that, Jamie went to Northeastern University for her master's in college student development and counseling and for the past three years she has been working at the University of New Hampshire overseeing the Fraternity and Life community there.

Feel free to browse the topics below to learn about what she offers, and how she can help YOU make a lasting impact on others! All programs can be in person or virtual, keynotes or facilitated program.

More information: www.greekuniversity.org/jamie

CHAPTER 6

A Sunday Talk on Sex, Drugs, Drinking, and Dying

Dr. Louis Profeta

Most bowed their heads or held their hands across their mouths as I described how it would happen. I told them that they will awaken with the smell of shit filling their bedroom. The lights will probably be low and the shades pulled and, because they are just waking up, they might have trouble focusing their eyes, especially after a night of heavy partying.

"Damn it, Benny, did you fart or shit yourself?" they might yell out. "Fucking get out of here, you smell awful!"

Those are the words I told them that they might shout just before they flip on the lights or stumble out of bed and trip on the now blue and stiff body sporting a college T-shirt passed down from an older brother who graduated two years past.

Dead, waxy, with "rock-still" clouded eyes, you could never envision a stare so distant. You played pickup basketball yesterday at the campus rec center and Benny maybe hit one out of ten threes. You blew him crap all day about it. Now, though, he is so still, laying among the pile of yet-to-be-washed clothes or wrapped up in a blanket on a piss-soaked IKEA futon delivered to him last week. You bought the TV and the coffee table. The top two drawers are yours.

"Think about it. Nobody gets up in the morning, brushes their teeth, combs their hair and says to themselves, 'Today is the day I die,'" I told them.

This was the second time I had given this talk—one I wish I could give to college students across the country as campuses now return to life. My son's fraternity at Indiana University-Bloomington, a Big Ten school and my alma mater housed in limestone buildings in an impossibly picturesque college town, had invited me to sit in front of more than two dozen young men in the living room of their fraternity. It was the most beautiful of Sunday afternoons. They could have been doing anything else. They did not have to be here, but here they were.

So I walked them through it. I showed them how I would tell their mom and dad that they were dead. "Oh trust me, it's not like what you see on TV. The doc in his white coat, breaking the news to the stoic father in the hallway while the mom softly sobs on his shoulders as he then asks the doctor some questions. For the sake of gender authenticity, how about I play the role of your father."

And I screamed.

I screamed and I screamed like a father in the deepest darkest throes of grief and despair, a sound so haunting that only those who do this for a living can truly understand its authenticity. Over and over I screamed the words "my son, my son . . . oh dear god, not my baby boy . . ."

And just as quick I stopped and I looked at them in a quiet voice, startling in its transformation and said, "Yeah, it kinda sounds like that. Do you have any fucking idea how selfish that is of you? Your parents will never be the same again, they will never be happy again. That is what love looks like. That is what love looks like."

And their heads stayed bowed and their hands covered their faces as they fought the urge to cry.

I described to them how Mom would pull hunks of her hair out 'til it bled and Dad would punch the wall shattering a bone or two but not noticing, a river of snot pouring from his face. I described how his "brothers" from the frat would sit along the wall in the waiting room and sob. But, already, Mom and Dad would be blaming them for getting their kid drunk or stoned to the point puke bubbled up in his throat, then plugged his trachea, choking him just as surely as if they had taken their foot and crushed their child's windpipe on their own.

"They will blame you for their child's death until the day you die. Are you ready for that?" I asked.

They sat silent.

I spent a few minutes pretending to breathe like someone asleep under the influence of a large amount of alcohol or just a few sedatives but who was at real risk of aspirating vomit into their lungs, or choking on their own tongue as it falls to the back of their mouth. You could tell from the look on their faces they all knew someone who once breathed like that after passing out drunk and now they were wondering how close they might have come, how close.

I challenged them with how absolutely idiotic it was for them to think that, just because they had perhaps taken a first-aid class or read a what-to-do-with-a-drunk-friend primer on the internet they somehow now had the skill set to "monitor" a friend who passed out after the fifth vodka slammer.

"We use well-trained nurses, paramedics, sophisticated pulse oximetry, and cardiac monitoring in our ER to assess these patients, not some pledge vying to become a 'brother.'" And they listened, and they listened intently. You could tell they wanted to know, and each one knew they needed to know.

"If you drink to the point that you do not have control of your faculties, you are an idiot. If you encourage someone to get to that point, you are an asshole and certainly no brother. Friends don't do that. It takes one little mistake to ruin your life or someone else's life forever." The room stayed quiet for a bit, but you could tell they wanted to ask more questions.

"You guys have a chance to ask me anything you want. You've got an ER doc who practices in a level I trauma center and who is on the board of directors of a major metropolitan city crime lab standing right in front of you. What do you want to know?"

And the hands finally went up—I should have known better; you could tell they needed a bit of a break.

"What about Viagra, is it safe for people our age?" Nervous laughter erupted.

"Son, which part of erection lasting more than six hours don't you understand?"

"Doc, that's the whole point."

"You're twenty-one and in college. You have Tinder, for God's sake. If you can't get an erection now, you've got a hell of a lot bigger problems than are fixable with Viagra. Besides, you know what we have to do for an erection lasting six hours? It's called priapism and its treatment involves two large needles . . ." A collective groan of thirty men a few years removed from puberty filled the room.

"What about Red Bull?" another hand shot up.

"It's just a boatload of caffeine; I've never understood mixing it with vodka. I guess if you like the taste, but what's the point of mixing a stimulant and a sedative? Seems like a waste of good vodka to me, but I feel the same about Jack and Coke. It's too easy to drink too much. Just . . . think about maybe not."

"What about Ativan?"

"Mix it with alcohol of any kind and you got a decent chance of dying. Why do you need to pass out? What the hell are you doing with it anyway? That's just stupid. If you are going to have a few drinks, then do that. If you are going to smoke some weed . . . well that's one thing, but don't fuck with prescription or non-prescription medications."

"Can you tell us about cocaine?"

"Yeah, use it once and you can die of a heart attack or have a stroke, then you can spend the rest of your life in a nursing home with a feeding tube poking out of your stomach, in a diaper, limbs contracted, getting huge bed sores and urine infections. You are out of your fucking mind if you use that. The same goes with heroin. You stand a good chance of dying or ending up brain damaged with even one single use. You guys need to kick out of your house anyone ever caught doing that shit. It's horribly addictive, life-destroying garbage. I have never, ever met a person that was glad they started using it . . . even once. And you are now one degree of separation away from the worst criminal element on earth."

"What about vaping?"

"It's better than smoking."

"What about Adderall?"

"It's a stimulant too, it's an amphetamine, you know like meth."

"Yeah, but nobody does that here—"

"Bullshit, pal," I interrupted and snapped back. "This is the Midwest. Memphis has barbecue. We make meth. Besides you probably don't have ADD; just try sleeping earlier, on occasion open a book and pay attention for a change." More than a few snickered.

"I'm not here to preach about all the evils of sex, drugs, weed, and alcohol to you. I'm not going to tell you to abstain, but just some food for thought. Studies clearly show though that your long-term earning potential will be less if you smoke weed on a regular basis. For that reason alone, I'd probably think twice, unless of course your lifelong dream is to always work for someone else. Weed typically doesn't open doors in your life. Drink, but think about perhaps not getting drunk. Have sex, but have responsible sex based on mutual understanding and respect. If you have to think about whether or not it's the right thing to do, then it's the wrong thing to do. Doing the right thing is simply not that confusing. It may be hard to do, but it's not that confusing."

"I'm a parent," I said, as I motioned to my child who seemed proud that I was there and I was proud that he asked me. "I want you to have a great college experience that helps prepare you for a long, healthy, and happy future. We understand each other?" They nodded. "You can always call me or one of my partners, or go to any ER in America if you need help or are scared or confused or worried or lost. Don't make me go into that quiet room, kneel in front of your mother, and tell her you're dead . . . please." They all nodded one final time.

And I could tell, on this sunny Sunday afternoon, that they were listening and that what I said mattered to them and it gave me hope. It gave me hope.

Dr. Louis M. Profeta is a nationally recognized, award-winning writer, TED Talk speaker, and Emergency Physician at St. Vincent Hospital of Indianapolis, a level 1 trauma center. He has cared for more than 60,000 patients. He is the best-selling author of the critically acclaimed book *The Patient in Room Nine Says He's God*. He is a dynamic and sought-after public speaker and frequent guest on TV and radio. He has gained critical acclaim for his poignant essays and writings for *LinkedIn Pulse Magazine* on topics such as our national heroin crisis in *When the Lion Kills Your Child*, end-of-life care in *I Know You Love Me Now Let Me Die*, and dozens of similar essays. In 2015, 2016, and 2017 he was named LinkedIn Top Voice for readership in health care. His scathingly sarcastic but passionate essay *Your Kid and My Kid Aren't Playing in the Pros* was honored as one of the best articles on sports by the Society of Professional

Journalism. In 2018, he was honored by the National Society of Newspaper Columnists for outstanding contribution to online media. His essays entitled *A Sunday Talk on Sex, Drugs, Drinking, and Dying* and *A Very Dangerous Place for a Child Is College* may be the most read and shared essays in history on the topic of drugs, sexual assault, and alcohol abuse on college campuses, having been read by millions. His 2018 essay *I'll Look at Your Facebook Profile Before I Tell Your Mother You're Dead* has become one of the most read articles in the world on social media.

Following the success of *A Sunday Talk on Sex, Drugs, Drinking, and Dying*, Dr. Profeta has been invited to speak all over the country on this topic. Dr. Profeta has told hundreds of parents their children have been killed over his career and he brings this reality to campuses across America. Some have described this as the most brutal, realistic, and impactful presentation ever given on the topic. He is rapidly becoming recognized as one of the most widely read opinion essayists in America today, including LinkedIn Top Voice in Health Care in 2020.

More information: www.greekuniversity.org/louis

CHAPTER 7

Captivated by Purpose vs. Comparison: Social Media and How We Measure Self-Worth

Cassie Firebaugh

As a former NFL cheerleader, I spent a lot of time during my earlier years comparing myself to others. I guess it came with the territory—and the cowboy boots. In fact, if I am completely transparent, I still find myself doing so from time to time. Even though I have a long list of accomplishments of my own from which to be proud of, I still have tons of moments scrolling though Instagram where I often feel inferior and insecure. My self-confidence is shaken as I compare myself to other women especially—from their outward appearance to their seemingly ideal relationships . . . from their vacation photos and even their ideal parenting skills. I forget about my own "highlight reel" and get swept away in someone else's. Although there have been countless moments where I catch myself having a pity party after fifteen minutes spent on social media, there is one snapshot of time that I believe was meant to challenge my perspective and provide an opportunity for self-growth and introspection.

I remember my thirty-ninth birthday looming ahead like a huge pimple brewing right before a formal event. I knew it was coming and it was the last one in my thirties and— just ugh . . . 40. Gross. I was officially going be "old." Even though I had worked hard to exercise, eat right, watch the wine, and was in the best shape of my life, I still felt like my youth was escaping me. I was so wrapped up in the number itself and felt my insecurity rising like cake batter as 3/7/18 was approaching.

Looking back, I should have been concerned about a whole separate set of numbers.

You see, 42 minutes after I put my 3 kids to bed, I had 1 moment that would change my life forever.

While sitting with my fiancé I suddenly felt a massive headache come on. I had a history of migraines with vision loss dating back to my childhood, so at first I thought this was just another one. I tried to stand up to get a glass of water and couldn't move. The entire left side of my body had gone numb. He could see the fear in my eyes as I tried to get the words out. However the droopiness of my mouth had set in and they came out jumbled.

"I think I am having a stroke."

As we raced to get to the hospital, I knew time was so critical. Little did I know just how critical. I have since learned you have less than 60 minutes from the moment the symptoms set in to be able to get treatment that can be lifesaving. Once a stroke begins, you lose almost 2 million brain cells every minute.

But all I could think of were the most important numbers of all.

My 3 kids were 11, 8, and 8. My soon-to-be stepchildren were 15, 14, and 13. I was 1 daughter of 2 amazing parents. I was 1 sister to 2 boys I had watched grow into strong men. And I was engaged to another incredible man who was 1 in a million.

And suddenly I realized I only had this 1 life . . . and so many reasons to fight for it.

After many hours of testing, the doctors discovered I had a small hole in my heart that had allowed for a clot to escape and make its way to settle in the right side of my brain. This is the side that controls language, attention, reasoning, and memory. It also is responsible for our creativity and artistic sense and, for someone like me who had built a life and business around those attributes, this was especially hard to imagine losing.

A few days later I went home more scared than I have ever been. Every little ache stressed me out—and even though the doctors threw out another set of numbers and statistics that back-to-back stroke occurrences are rare, I couldn't shake the feeling it would happen again.

I was right. Two weeks after my first stroke I was in the kitchen making a smoothie and suddenly my hands went clumsy and I dropped it all over the floor. NO way this was happening again. What are the chances? Well they are 1 in 4, and I was the exception.

That July I went in for the procedure to address what I came to know as Patent Foramen Ovale syndrome—or PFO, for short. As I drifted off into a deep sleep on the operating table, I remember making a promise to God and myself that the moment I woke up on the other side of this that I would never take for granted the gift of my life. That I would be less concerned about what strangers on social media (or in real life) thought of me and more about the faces that flashed in front of me in the moments I was being rushed to the hospital fighting for my life.

Yet, hours later as I was lying in recovery, I found myself compelled to write a post to alert all 3K of my "friends" and family that I had suffered two strokes but was—God willing—going to be okay. I hesitated for a moment—because this was very intimate news about my health, after all—but my need to feel connected, and what I viewed at the time as supported, eventually won out. Some may wonder . . . why? Why did she feel she had to share something so personal with so many strangers?

Humans are social creatures, and science tells us that social interactions are necessary for our physical and mental wellness. If living through a pandemic has taught us anything, it is how much we have taken for granted the person-to-person connections that are vital to the health of our humanity as a whole. Now more than ever we are forced to limit these face-to-face interactions and instead take to social media in order to fulfill the need to feel connected to others. However, Instagram Envy is arguably now a modern-day pandemic in itself, presenting its own contagious and dangerous complications that can contribute to disease states such as mental illness, depression, and anxiety. We travel, eat, and sleep next to our phones in case of an urgent notification—or even non-urgent updates from a stranger. We gorge on bitesize updates on other people's lives—regardless of whether we're still in close contact with them or not. We feel pressure to present a perfected version of ourselves online, only to feel worse offline in our own reality. It is no doubt that social media is now, unfortunately, an unstoppable force. We crave the desire to be in the know—or be known. We tend to get so caught up in comparison that we lose sight of being captivated by our unique and individual purpose.

As we continue to engage in a world driven by online interaction, we must be dedicated to adopting and creating a healthy approach to social media—and therefore the standards in which we judge ourselves and our peers. But how does one even begin to start this process?

Set Healthy Boundaries and Stay ACCOUNTable

It has been proven that short but frequent scrolling sessions, known as passive consumption, are when we are most subconsciously absorbent. This is important when we consider how Instagram's algorithm prioritizes the content that you interact with most. Whether that be through likes, messages, or a guilty stalk here and there, the accounts you gravitate toward will naturally reappear more on your feed. Unfortunately research indicates we are more likely to see and remember the accounts that have a detrimental effect on our mental well-being.

We all have certain things, or people, in our lives that can trigger insecurities. And while it will largely be unavoidable to eliminate in entirety, we can make choices every day that build our confidence rather than tear it down. Being honest with yourself about which accounts can perhaps trigger a negative emotional response is a crucial factor toward achieving healthy boundaries. Limiting online activity, or perhaps muting the accounts that contribute to Instagram Envy when at our most vulnerable moments, is something we can do keep ourselves grounded when confronted with social pressures that threaten our sense of self-worth and confidence. Only when we take time to reflect on our mind-set with raw honesty can we can follow the right path in how we approach it for the best chance for overall mental health and happiness.

No One's Life Is as Perfect as Their Instagram Feed

Don't let people "influence" you to believe otherwise.

Social media comparison is at scary, scary levels. So the question is: How can we preserve our mental wellness and increase our own confidence without constant comparison or competition with our peers?

Today we are behind the wheel of a vehicle that allows us to create our own stories—"create" being the operative word. I am able to manipulate reality in a way that it benefits "me." The obvious problem with this is that anyone who is following you is seeing your highlight reel, and, in turn, comparing their lives to yours. This is not dangerous alone, but coupled with the pressure to keep up the illusion that life is all lemonade without the lemons (or even sugar or calories!), this can lead to a detrimental crash for one's self esteem. The domino effect of hearts and comments can quickly push jealousy and envy which magnifies insecurities—and at times stealthily threatens real-life relationships (innocently or otherwise) to tumble. A vicious circle ensues as we gravitate toward posting our highlight reels to make our life seem more sweet than sour—giving us a form of vanity validation. This, in turn, often leads to peer pressure that fosters insane fear of missing out (FOMO) and so the cycle repeats itself. We devour certain Instagram feeds and desire to be them or have what they do. We see what we perceive as "perfect" lives and consequently feel terrible about our own because it doesn't measure up. Our wellness suffers and stalls.

However, more often than not, there is a disconnect between what we see in person and what we see online—or at least that is not the entire picture—as pretty as it is. The irony is we measure the success of our peers through an illusory "point" system that unfavorably punishes us and rewards others. As we start to compare we allow our special moments to be overshadowed by someone else's moment which we now view as more special, when in reality we have our pretty damn enviable ones too—they just don't always make it to a reel or feed. Once we allow ourselves to do this, our happiness and joy is diminished or taken away completely. The key to lasting fulfillment of your own life is learning how to not only accept, but embrace that it's okay to "miss out" on what we think we want. It's better than okay—it's a beautiful thing to be in our own moments—and carve our own path.

Identify the Influences We Choose vs. Manipulations We Do Not

Seemingly gone are the days of runway models flaunting lingerie and high-end clothing or a middle-aged housewife selling the latest and greatest gadget for the home. Out with snooty modeling agencies and in with trendy and well-connected twenty-somethings who have given birth to the brand sponsorship dubbed "the influencer" (however, when introduced in the same tone as The Terminator I can't help but laugh a little). Companies hire influencers based on their follower count and equate the ability to essentially sell their service or product like actors in a commercial. However, this is not a stranger on TV appealing to our needs and desires . . . it is our trusted friend or coworker. It's personal. Relatable. It's marketing ingenuity. It's easy to lose control of your time, energy, and money trying to emulate someone else's identity or trick yourself into believing if you just had what they did then you would be happy or _____ too. The reality is, there is not a single item that can be purchased or idea that can be replicated that will ensure a solid sense of self-worth other than the work you invest in within yourself.

So with this in mind, as an individual who doesn't feel she can be easily bought, in addition to being a parent of teens, I was horrified while watching the Netflix documentary *The Social Dilemma*. I went to bed feeling manipulated and used as a pawn by the kings of huge social media platforms to further their financial game of chess. On the other side of the board, I was angry at myself for making it so easy to be played. Everything from our vulnerabilities and desires for connection to tempting our need to be more (so buy more) is fair play. Sadly, social media accountability is not going to change anytime soon—in fact, it will only continue to worsen. Therefore, we need to be able to disseminate between what we are openly making the choice to allow into our minds— and what is slyly trying to be snuck in through the side door. More times than not our feed is carefully curated to prey on our individual emotional desires and needs—be it through social engagement or financial spending. However, keep in mind you control the doors here—open and close them wisely.

Turn Social Stress to Self-Love Success

Let's get comfortable with the fact we can't edit our real-life stories with the click of a button or swipe of a filter. Some parts are raw. Ugly, filled with true emotional ups and downs and maybe would never make our "highlight reel." But they are also genuine and beautiful and make you uniquely who you are. As unglamorous as it sounds, mine might simply be my girls asking for one more back rub while I tuck them in, even though I'm dying to just flop my weary mom bones into the couch and watch *Yellowstone* after a long day. Or maybe it's my son out on the basketball court doing what he loves, hitting the 3-pointer and as he glances in my direction, my eyes would be ready to meet his instead of perhaps missing it because I was trying to get my own "perfect shot" for an Instagram-worthy moment. Don't wait for a life-altering moment like a stroke to remind yourself that you are witnessing the most beautiful and authentic story unfold right in front of your eyes. We don't need perfect skin and hair or a gorgeous partner on a romantic weekend getaway to prove our beauty or value. So what if our peer gets a better grade or lucrative job offer? Are all of those things nice? Yep. Is it okay to want them or even crave the actual new pair of shoes someone on social media is wearing in addition to the path they are walking which seems destined to lead to happiness and success?

Absolutely.

Does it mean that the very life we have in front of us—imperfections and all—are any less meaningful or valuable?

Absolutely not.

We spend so much time building others up with a "heart" here or a "like" there. However, when was the last time you shifted the focus on "liking" the most important person and life out there—you and your own? When did you last find yourself praising your accomplishments and successes without comparing them to someone else's? If you're like most, more effort needs to be spent on cultivating your own identity and self-esteem. Focus on embracing and nourishing the relationships with people who see the real you in all the chapters of your story—the pretty parts as well as the broken ones. The faces of tried-and-true, real friendships who help us hold steady to our truest beliefs who believe in us. Sometimes we just need to put the screen down and choose to look up. Whether it's into the eyes of those seated next to you at a dinner table or perhaps simply finding gratitude as you glance around the room at the ones who are sharing the same four walls you do in that moment.

We all have the ability to leave an imprint on this world and a voice to be heard . . . be proud of yours and never lose sight of the meaning each individual chapter adds to the story of your life.

Cassie Firebaugh joins us from Indianapolis, Indiana, and this former NFL cheerleader (Go Colts!) is no stranger to the challenges the game of life throws her way. As a busy mom of six, business owner, and entrepreneur, it's safe to say she definitely has a few balls of her own to keep in the air!

However, that very full life came to a screeching halt one evening as she experienced a stroke on her birthday that changed everything. Against the odds, two weeks later she had a second one. Cassie has tackled many obstacles such as living with a heart defect, single motherhood, and multiple business creation and ownership. Today as her story continues, she is living proof that you can turn pain and fear into power and fuel. Cassie is passionate about using her voice to inspire students to confidently stand up and use their own to speak to be heard.

Her love for all things Greek is deeply rooted in her time at Indiana University-Bloomington where she was a member of the Beta chapter of Pi Beta Phi. Cassie also has served as a Panhellenic representative and is beyond excited to continue this journey. She will not only engage students with her humor and heart, but offer impactful programs for the development of empowered leaders throughout campus and beyond.

More information: www.greekuniversity.org/cassie

CHAPTER 8

Men, Masculinity, and Being Our Authentic Selves

Joseph Thompson

A s I thought about writing this chapter, it was difficult not to reflect on the circumstances under which I am doing so. We are amid a global pandemic where countless lives have been lost, folks are without work, and most of us have a feeling of uncertainty regarding the future. I seldom leave my house other than for groceries, but when I do I have to wear a mask to protect myself and others. I am still working, but cannot help but empathize for those who have lost their jobs due to COVID-19. Still, I am positive for the future.

Almost one year has passed since the beginning of the pandemic, and yet one "debate" still carries on—whether to wear a mask when leaving the house. While this may seem like an irrelevant topic if you are reading this beyond the conclusion of the coronavirus outbreak, it serves as an example of the type of behavior relevant to study of masculinity and our behaviors. As I write this, men account for almost 70% of US deaths related to COVID-19,[6] yet men are also far less likely to wear masks or "social-distance" than women.[7] Research shows it may be misplaced notions of manliness that is motivating US men to ignore experts' guidance. One such study from the peer-reviewed journal *Behavioral Science & Policy* found women are more likely to report embracing expert-backed behaviors such as wearing a mask and social distancing.[8] A similar study found that men were more likely to see masks as a sign of weakness or "uncool."[9] Why is it that men cannot see past these unhealthy ideas of masculinity and realize it is literally going to kill them?

In this chapter, I will seek to provide an answer to that question as well as how we can individually challenge the social constructs of traditional masculinity in order to live happier, healthier lives.

---

[6] Jian-Min Kin, Peng Bai, Wei He, Fei Wu, Xiano-Fang Liu, De-Min Han, Shi Liu, and Jin-Kui Yang (2020) "Gender Differences in Patients with COVID-19: Focus on Severity and Mortality," *Frontiers in Public Health*, https://www.frontiersin.org/articles/10.3389/fpubh.2020.00152/full.

[7] Irmak O. Okten et al., "Gender Differences in Preventing the Spread of Coronavirus," Behavioral Science & Policy Association, October 4, 2020. Retrieved from https://behavioralpolicy.org/journal_issue/covid-19?.

[8] Ibid.

[9] Valerio Capraro and Helene Barcelo, "The Effect of Messaging and Gender on Intentions to Wear a Face Covering to Slow Down COVID-19 Transmission" (May 11, 2020). Retrieved from https://doi.org/10.31234/osf.io/tg7vz).

Masculinity as a Social Construct

I do an exercise with students that asks them to define masculinity—that is, what do they perceive as masculine characteristics? If you think about this for a moment, you would probably come up with ideas like strength, athleticism, courage, independence, leadership, and assertiveness. While models of masculinity have changed over time and differ from culture to culture, power and dominance tend to be common themes across most.[10] It is our culture and society that upholds a constrained view of what masculinity "should be." We come across these ideas through our socialization and it becomes "normal" or "natural" to us. This hegemonic view of masculinity becomes the default and anything different is therefore not masculine. Alas, when I do the exercise above, most people come up with similar definitions of masculinity. Our socialization tells us a "normal guy" lives a very specific lifestyle and we should strive to model that behavior . . . or so I even thought.

When I was a teenager, like most, I was insecure. I was skinny, and while I played multiple sports, I was never incredibly athletic. I certainly did not have natural talent as an athlete. I slowly gave up several sports I played, until high school, when I decided to stick with ice hockey. I was always jealous of other guys around me who seemed in better shape, had more muscle, and were more athletic. These insecurities were not just about being on the ice and my ability to be a star athlete, however. As a teenage guy thinking about girls

---

[10] R. W. Connell and James W. Messerschmidt, "Hegemonic Masculinity: Rethinking the Concept," *Gender & Society* 19, No. 6 (December 1, 2005), 829–59.

and popularity, it was more nerve-wracking to walk around high school halls. How do I compete with these other guys who looked like they should play the varsity quarterback in a movie? How did some of the guys I know have biceps and six-packs at age seventeen? I could understand the pressure that led some guys to try steroids . . . or just the opposite— quit athletic activity altogether. Whether we want to believe it or not, as men we compare ourselves to other men and it starts young. What pushed me to work harder on the ice was also what made me insecure and unhappy.

Playing hockey aside, I did not really care to watch sports on television until I was well into college. It might seem funny to some, but this was another area of insecurity. As a guy, why didn't I want to watch sports? Why didn't I watch every game and memorize stats like a lot of the guys around me? I even went as far as lying to friends in high school when they asked if I "watched the game." I was helping to hold up masculine norms by pretending to enjoy doing something I really did not at the time.

Sports, however, was not the subject that made me the most insecure and pressured though. Like many straight high school and college guys, the subject most on my mind was girls. If sports is not your thing, perhaps you can relate to this.

I can't remember the first time I listened to other guys talk about sex, but I can remember how uncomfortable I felt around it in general. While true or just fabrications, guys around me would talk about who they hooked up with and what sexual acts they engaged in. They spoke about girls in a way that treated them like objects, particularly in how they engaged in sexual acts. There was a one-upmanship regarding the number of girls they hooked up with and what they did.

I didn't care for these conversations. I had a girlfriend for most of high school and I certainly didn't want to treat her as an object of teenage conquest, but to say there was no outside pressure for me to have sex would be a lie. Guys would ask me about it as if it were their business, and they did so in the crudest way possible. At the time, that was just normal to me—even if I didn't participate. It was just another thing at the time I brushed off, as if *boys will be boys*.

Ultimately, I did feel pressured though. It was difficult not to. While I had no intention of sharing details of my personal life with anyone, when I finally did have sex, I wanted to tell other guys. But, why? Why did I feel the need to suddenly share these intimate details? I guess I needed to be like them. I needed to feel like one of the boys. I was presented with two opposing feelings: pride and shame. Proud because sex is somehow an accomplishment, and shame because I felt that way.

As men we need to stop comparing ourselves to other men. Whether it be in our careers, daily lives, or relationships. We don't have to feel shame or less than if we haven't had sex, or multiple partners, or have a relationship. We need to take that stress off ourselves.

My experiences around relationships and sex has taught me a lot about masculinity. As a married man in my thirties now, I still reflect back on my own experiences and how it has shaped me. Today I can say that I am happier than I have ever been—not just because I am married to someone I love, but also because those experiences growing up taught me to ignore those outside pressures as much as I could and to have healthier relationships.

How Traditional Masculinity Can Be Harmful

While pretending to watch every football game was not necessarily harmful, other masculine-seeking behaviors can be. As a fraternity/sorority advisor on a college campus now, I think about alcohol abuse, hazing, rape culture, mental health issues, and other harmful outcomes that may be rooted in unhealthy models of masculinity.

Let me start personally by talking about mental health issues as an outcome of hegemonic masculinity. Being insecure about sex and my athleticism was not the end of my high school woes. Comparing myself to others and feeling like I could not live up to societal expectations I placed on myself led me down a path to issues with anxiety and depression I still face today. For many, this is exacerbated by the fact that men are less likely to seek mental health care or doctors at all. The American Psychological Association released guidelines in 2018 for working with men and boys for that very reason.[11]

---

[11] American Psychological Association, Boys and Men Guidelines Group. (2018). APA guidelines for psychological practice with boys and men. Retrieved from http://www.apa.org/about/policy/psychological-practice-boys-men-guidelines.pdf.

Men are often taught showing emotions is a sign of weakness, so while I grew up dealing with my anxiety and insecurities, I hid them. My emotions were private to me. They caused me to spend a lot of time alone, dwelling on them, brooding. Emotional restriction like this is linked to increased negative risk-taking and aggression—and I showed plenty of it. My depression turned to rage and self-harm. Contemplating suicide was not foreign to me.

Eventually I received the help I needed, through therapy and doctors. I hope anyone reading this knows it is okay, and even normal to seek help for mental health. Seeking help is not a sign of weakness. It's a sign of being human. Just like our physical health, we need to take care of ourselves. I just hope it's normalized for all boys and men someday so that others don't have continue turning to more negative ways of coping.

While I was able to get help, a lot of other men in similar situations may turn to drugs or alcohol as coping mechanisms. Men also may abuse alcohol as a result of these narrow expectations of masculinity. A large body of evidence indicates that social drinking is a primary cultural symbol of manliness.[12] As a college administrator myself, I think it is important to understand this as it relates to students' alcohol consumption and potential abuse. That is, alcohol abuse may be a symptom of a greater concern—of men's ability to meet the demands of societal expectations of manhood. In no way am I saying consuming alcohol is necessarily a negative behavior. I enjoy a craft beverage or two myself. It is

---

[12] Russell Lemle & Marc E. Mishkind, "Alcohol and Masculinity," *Journal of Substance Abuse Treatment* 6, Issue 4 (January 1, 1989), 213–22.

the way we drink and the amount we drink as a society that is concerning, particularly in college-aged men.

Maybe archaic expectations of masculinity are the root cause of men's drinking behaviors, and if we can tackle the root cause, perhaps the negative behaviors will slowly subside? I would make the same argument for hazing and other negative behaviors we see in college men in particular—even rape culture. Perhaps they are the results of toxic beliefs about being a man we have been socialized to believe, engrained in us subconsciously over time. Whether we choose to act on them or act against them is on us. We must take responsibility for our actions regardless of external pressure. When a man feels entitled to assault someone, he may get drunk before he does it, but the decision to act was ultimately his own.

Reflecting on my time in high school being pressured to have sex and tell other guys when I did was considered normal to me at the time—and ultimately normal meant healthy, right? Sharing that information was ultimately my own, and I am glad I did not bend to the pressure. Had I though, I would have contributed to the toxic environment that often permeates around men and sex, contributing to the rape culture that exists in our society. It would not just have affected me, but my sexual partner too. That is not something I thought about then, but now that I am older it is easier to reflect on those situations and understand the pressure I was going through. These situations are not uncommon for boys and men. They can be harmful to us and those involved.

Being Our Authentic Selves

Some folks reading this might believe they are completely independent, void of outside influence or societal expectations of them—but that is entirely unrealistic. As humans we are socialized to conform to norms. We want to fit in. We want to be liked and accepted. As a result, the image we present to the world may not be our own. There is no better example of that than our social media. Do you post photos of yourself the moment you wake up in bed? Probably not. You wait until you feel you look good. We all do it. So how do we reflect on our behaviors and start to live a life of authenticity?

First, we need to work on our self-awareness. Focus on your thoughts and actions. What forces are helping you make decisions? Can you objectively evaluate yourself? Do your behaviors align with your values? Often how we perceive ourselves and how others perceive us vary. It can be very difficult to separate these two, as that is the very definition of being self-aware. There are often behaviors I still have that are reflective of masculine norms. Not all are negative, they are simply masculine norms. It's important I understand where my behaviors originated. Using an example I shared above, I was raised to not treat women as sexual objects but I was also surrounded by media and people who often did. Was I going to follow my values or my need to fit in?

We also need self-acceptance. No one is perfect. We need to accept our own flaws and deficiencies. We also need to accept what makes us unique and different than those around us. Accept your talents and capabilities too. What you perceive as good or bad about yourself are still things that make you,

you. I have accepted the fact that I am not the most athletic man in the world, but that does not have to stop me from hitting the gym either. I still find myself comparing myself to other men, but I am now empowered to acknowledge it and still be happy with who I am. I am a work in progress, but we all are.

The whole idea of what a real man is supposed to be, or what is masculine or not, is ever-changing, and therefore nonsense. The only person we should compare ourselves to is our old self. Am I growing? Am I striving to always do better? To be better? Am I being true to myself and my values?

Authenticity is being the man you want to be.

Am I man the man I want to be?

I am working on it.

Joseph Thompson is a student affairs professional with 8+ years' experience focusing on furthering the fraternity/sorority movement, facilitating student leadership and personal development, and advocating social justice issues. He is the Assistant Director of Student Development at Stockton University.

Joseph has a master's degree in college student affairs from Rutgers University, and a bachelor's degree in history and secondary education from Susquehanna University. Joseph is a brother of Phi Mu Delta Fraternity and is currently serving as the National Treasurer.

More information: www.greekuniversity.org/joseph

CHAPTER 9

Healthy Relationships Take Work: Are You Willing to Do What It Takes?

Tricia Benitez

ate yourself!! Let's dive a little further into this. Several years ago, right after I left an extremely toxic relationship, I was scared to death, lonely, felt ashamed, and embarrassed. I then finally listened to several of my peers and coworkers who understood the situation and I sought out therapy through my company's employee assistance program. Let me just tell you, the first two months at therapy I sat in front of my therapist . . . I couldn't even murmur a word and bawled my eyes out. After she peeled back several layers of my insecurity, the largest piece of advice that she gave me was to "date myself." Completely bewildered by this new concept I asked her, "What on earth should I do?"

She then asked me how I like my coffee, and I sat there and thought about it and realize that for many years I was not doing anything I truly liked. For instance, if somebody liked caramel macchiato, that's what I would order. To my fellow readers, I strongly encourage you to do this regardless of your relationship status because it helps build a strong foundation. One of the very first things I did was went to a coffee shop and ordered my favorite coffee. In fact, I ordered an extra large dirty chai iced latte. After the barista handed me my luscious beverage, I took myself to a table, not in the corner, but where I could be seen. I sat there very nervously at first drinking MY coffee. The first time I did this it only lasted about five minutes and I got super nervous. My palms got sweaty, I got up and left. I felt like I was weird and awkward because I was sitting there alone and I didn't know how to just be.

After many more months of therapy and many more mini self-dates, I went for the big one! I took myself out to Ruth's Chris Steak House. I had a full meal all by myself and I was so happy and excited to experience enjoying my own company. Even after having heard "Oh only you??" from the hostess, I joked right back with her and said "Oh I hope it is only one because I couldn't handle two of me tonight!" I hope this first bit of advice resonates with some, if not many, to go experience things that you genuinely want to do. You don't need anyone's permission to love who you are. You don't need anyone's permission to do the things that you genuinely love doing. Go ahead and give yourself permission to go on a date with YOU!

Put down the phone! Listen to who you're with—to understand, not to respond. Have you ever noticed while in conversation with someone, although you are enjoying it, you're already thinking of how to respond all the while they're still talking? If you are, guess what, you're normal. We are all guilty of this. However, what this is telling is that you're already tuned out of what they are still saying and already anticipating jumping in with the answer or an interjection of your opinion. Next time you're talking with someone and you realize that you're already thinking of the answer before they finish speaking, stop yourself. Pause your mind, breathe, and re-engage with the person in front of you. This does take practice and no one is perfect. I definitely still interrupt people when I am very excited and engaged in the conversation, and I am working on this. When you pause and really listen, you will also see that the communications are much more meaningful. People love to be heard/validated, not interrupted. Speaking of interruptions, let's talk about having to stop a meal to take a picture to post it on social media. Or when the food comes, telling everyone they can't touch their food because you have to be the one who takes a picture to put it on social media followed by several different filtered selfies.

Not every moment needs to be shared on social media. Our world is so instant these days, leaving very little to the imagination. Very few things these days are actually sacred and kept personally to oneself. I am by no means suggesting never take a selfie or never post that gorgeous food picture.

However, a little change of pace is always good. How about a little challenge? Try not posting every single moment of your life online and instead make a journal entry for that night/date/event. Not only will this help you be more present with whoever you're with but it also gives you guys something really cool to revisit later. Putting down your phone and disconnecting with it could very well lead to a much more fundamental connection with the person you're actually with.

Say what you actually mean; mean what you actually say! I challenge you to actually own your crap! I'm not always right, and you are not always right either. Something else super valuable that I learned in therapy was how to calm your brain and get comfortable when the situation is uncomfortable. Why as humans do we not like to be uncomfortable or avoid challenging conversations? The answer is actually pretty simple. We are scared of confrontation, rejection, humiliation, and being vulnerable. One thing that has been very beneficial is understanding that it's not necessarily what you say, but it's the tone of which you say it in. A good tip is if you're unsure of how to say something, our phones can actually come in handy here. Go ahead and record you saying exactly how you're feeling it. Play it back a couple of times. If you feel that it could be offensive or misconstrued, that means it probably will be. If you still can't figure out the right tonality to say something, write it down. If it's something that's a very sensitive topic, I would suggest finding a way to talk about it rather than text. Whether we want to believe it or not, people do in fact put tonality behind a text message. A simple text can be completely taken the wrong way and cause discord for absolutely no reason. It's okay to agree to disagree. Sometimes people will battle with one another because they simply want to have their side of the argument validated and heard. All the while, not even giving the other person a moment of clarity. Meaning, the two people are going to constantly battle, battle, battle and get to no resolution. Not everyone is going to see eye to eye and your side of the story. That's okay. As frustrating as it can be, please keep in mind that some battles are just simply not worth showing up for. It's okay to go to bed angry/upset. Beating a dead horse won't make it any deader. In fact, it will cause a bigger problem than it ever should have. Sometimes tabling a topic, going to sleep, and waking up with a fresh mind will help to actually reflect back on the argument and realize how silly or unnecessary it was. It's okay to place your pride aside and apologize.

The scary T word . . . THERAPY. Let's normalize this! I'm coming right out and saying it: we are all a little broken, nobody's perfect, we are all deserving of love. Throughout life you'll meet many people and you'll hear their stories. Here's the secret—everyone has a story. It's not a competition of who has been through the worst trauma at all. My trauma could be very different from yours, that doesn't mean it's any worse than yours or vice versa. As a child, after being awarded to the state for some time, I got out but I had to go to therapy. Looking back on it now I am so thankful for that time. Had I not had the therapy, maybe I wouldn't be in the position I am today. My therapist later in life also told me that it's okay to cut people off even if that's a family member. Just because someone is related to you does not give them permission to abuse you. One of the hardest things I've ever said was "This is not okay, this is not healthy, I love you and right now I can't allow you in my life." Then I hung up! I was absolutely terrified after I did this.

The strangest thing though after I said that, my relationship with this family member became extremely different in a good way. Therapy taught me boundaries. Placing boundaries down is very scary and it'll make you very nervous, but it's so worth it. Therapy doesn't mean that you're weak, or you can't do it, or you're screwed up. It simply means that you need someone who has a non-biased opinion who studied endless hours who can give you the tools to place in your toolbox so you can embrace the challenges of life in a more healthy fashion. Fair warning though, not everybody will know how to accept this new you, and you may outgrow friends, people, and jobs. Guess what, that's okay. Fall in love with you! You owe it to you. Give yourself permission to look in the mirror and say *I am not the victim, I'm an amazing person, I am full of love, I was born for greatness!* It'll definitely seem silly at first but over time your relationship of any kind will absolutely benefit from you taking the initiative to be the best you, to show up, and be present.

On the other hand, if you are wishing that the person that you're either in a relationship with, a family member, a friend, or a spouse would go to therapy, then one of the most challenging things that I will write is this: *you cannot want it for them more than they want it for themselves.* I've done this before as well. If the person that you want to go to therapy refuses to go for whatever reason, you can always be the change that you want to see and start going alone by yourself. This has greatly helped many folks. At the end of the day you should pause, listen, and just be there. Sometimes that holds more weight than our "thoughts."

Finally, all relationships of any sort have their ups and downs. There are no perfect couples, there's no perfect siblings, no perfect parents, no perfect coworkers, no perfect friends, and no perfect acquaintances. The biggest piece of advice is listen to your gut. If something with someone does not feel right, there's a really big chance that it's not. For instance, going out to eat. If they are very rude to the serving staff, that's probably a huge sign that you should pay attention to! If someone constantly makes you question how you're dressing or where you're going, that's a very scary controlling, narcissistic sign. I hope you don't make the same mistake that I did, which was I gave that person an excuse and said "oh this was just one time." The reality is, that's literally who he was and it almost cost me my life. The people that call and check on you to see if you had enough to eat or if you just want some company, keep those people close. They are extremely special and rare.

If you are interested in someone and every single person that loves you or that is close to you is telling you that you shouldn't be with whoever that is, listen to them!! They are literally on the outside seeing all the red flags looking in and they're also seeing this stuff before it happens. Listen to them although it may feel as if they are being annoying or they don't want you to be happy. Several people who are around you and close to you would not all have the exact same opinion of one person if that one person hadn't triggered their gut reaction! I was extremely stubborn and although everybody told me I should not have dated the man who almost killed me, I ignored them. I pushed them away and I ended up leaving that relationship. Finally, it was with a gun pressed to my head. To sum this up, if someone makes you feel bad or belittles you, they are seriously not worth your time. Time is precious. It's the only thing money cannot buy. It's okay to be choosy about who you spend your time with. #loveyoumore

Tricia Benitez and her family were no strangers to addiction. Her father suffered from alcoholism, her mother admits to doing cocaine on several occasions, and her brother struggled for a long time with drugs. These active addictions were also noticed by the authorities. Tricia's mother left her when she was an infant, trying to give her away like a puppy to a distant family in Florida. Tricia's father had an addiction that resulted in Tricia being a taken away by the state as a child. Orphanage was the child's version of a jail. Tricia was fortunate to have a sister who was eighteen years older, and she had the ability to get Tricia out of the orphanage. Her sister played such an instrumental part of her life by helping to raise Tricia, as well as continuously being supportive of her career in the midst of a very dysfunctional family. Tricia's brother lost his battle from addiction, going in and out of treatment centers numerous times himself. On June 8, 2002, his landlord found him dead in his apartment due to a drug overdose.

Tricia's dad demonstrated how to live a gypsy life, so she found it "normal" to shack up with lots of people. In her early twenties, she found herself in a horrible relationship. Tricia ran away and turned to meth to escape. When she finally escaped, it was with a gun to her head, $100 to her name, four bags of clothes, and her dog named Pink.

Tricia has completely turned her life around since that day. Much of her time has been spent as a Treatment Specialist for Addiction Campuses in Nashville, Tennessee. There, she was on the front lines of the opioid epidemic and other forms of addiction as a resource for people to get help instead of landing in jail or worse. Tricia has helped almost 1,500 people get the help and treatment they need for their addictions over the last six years. Tricia shares her own powerful story of addiction and dysfunctional relationships with students all across the country to ensure that they get the help they need for themselves or others on their campus, as well as showing the students what a healthy relationship should look like.

More information: www.greekuniversity.org/tricia

CHAPTER 10

Confidence, Courage, and Mind-Set

Edson O'Neale

C onfidence, courage, and a good mind-set—three things needed not only in college but also in life. Everyone struggles with this at times. We tell ourselves that we can't do something and we continue the negative self-talk until we firmly believe it. We allow society to make us feel we are beneath ourselves; we allow society to dictate our happiness, therefore allowing us to feel we are not confident in ourselves. We do not have the courage to do what is necessary and to have the mind-set to achieve our goals.

Why is it so hard to get back up when you get kicked down? Why put yourself out there and push forward, when you can just simply throw in the towel and not have to worry about it? Why should you put in the time and effort? I will tell you why—because you will not be able to really see the truest version of who you are and what you are meant to be if you are not challenged.

The whole point of this chapter is to help someone realize that you are not alone and there are others who struggle internally through things, and that at any point when you are ready to take control you can make the necessary steps to do so.

Confidence: What Does It Mean to You?

Confidence can mean different things to different people. The dictionary term of confidence is the "feeling or belief that one can rely on someone or something, firm trust, a feeling of self-assurance from one's appreciation of one's own abilities or qualities." What confidence means to me is to firmly believe in yourself that once you put your mind to something, you can do it. Without confidence, it is hard to achieve your goals. I interviewed some of my colleagues to get their feedback on confidence and what it means to them:

- "Confidence is knowing your worth."—*Julenny Rodriguez* (senior at Saint Leo University)
- "There is a fine line between confidence and cockiness. Our future leaders need to be careful to not impose their confidence improperly to those they are serving."—*Shawn Livingstone* (Student Development at Pace University)
- "Having confidence is to love yourself enough to practice self-care. If you don't, you cannot find the balance to have the confidence it takes to lead and to feed confidence into others."—*Jarred Pernier*

(2nd year graduate student at the University of West Florida)

- "Having confidence is someone who walks into a room and they bring an energy that is palpable. Although, confidence can look different externally and internally—it is important they match and align with each other."—*Krystal Sanchez-Williams* (Director of Student Leadership, the University of Vermont)
- "Confidence is when others say you can't, and you tell them, 'Watch me . . .'"—Ana Didonato (mentor)

Courage: What Does It Mean to You?

Courage and confidence go hand in hand. In order to build confidence, you must develop the courage to do so. Courage is defined as the ability to do something that is frightening and having strength in the face of pain or grief. The courage to do what is right will always set you apart from anyone else. When others take the cowardly approach and the easy way out, you choose courage and stand up. I asked my colleagues again what does courage mean to them:

- "Standing up for what is right when no one else will."—*Jarred Pernier*
- "Being so sold out to what you believe in and willing to go against the grain."—*Shawn Livingstone*
- "Despite the what-if's, despite how you internally feel, despite how scared you are, you show up and you do it anyways."—*Krystal Sanchez-Williams*

- "Courage is also recognizing that you are allowed to be at the table, you are allowed to be in the room, and you are allowed to be part of conversation."— *James Robilatta* (award-winning speaker)

I want you to ask yourself something: *Am I courageous? Have I ever stood up for something that I knew was right even though others told me otherwise?* If your answer is no, guess what . . . it is okay. The fact that you are honest with yourself is courageous in itself, and it is never too late to make that decision to be courageous.

Mind-Set: What Does It Mean to You?

You can have confidence and courage, but if you do not develop the mind-set to put your confidence and courage together to push through, you will not be able to achieve your goals. I discussed "mind-set" with my colleagues and heard different takes on what was needed to develop a positive mind-set:

- "First and foremost, never plateau—it pushes you to do better." —*Shawn*
- "Everyone needs to have an ace partner: your ace partner will always keep you aware, check your attitude when it is not right, and will hold you accountable."—*Michael Cadore* (Associate Vice President at Florida Eastern University)
- "Your past situations that did not work out do not define who you are—it is okay to accept what

has happened and move forward."—*Hope Swaim* (Hall Director at Texas Christian University)

- "A positive mind-set is focused on service—serving and touching the lives of others."—*Ana Didonato*
- "You have to be the light in the dark room because when everything is dark, it is important to be the beacon of light that inspires others and to get people through a rough day." —*Jarred Pernier*

My Personal Experience

I have always struggled with confidence my whole life, and that struggle brought me to a place where I thought the world would be a better place if I wasn't in it. I cared more about what people thought of me than caring about myself, and that is something that I continue to struggle with.

It all really began in Junior High. I was bullied, made fun of, and never felt accepted. I thought college would bring me past those troubles. Yet I was in a very dark place mentally—I was always mad and just didn't care about my life.

During the first semester of my freshman year at college, I felt numb so to actually feel something that I would punch the wall until I cut myself, started bleeding, or put a hole in the wall because I just wanted to feel something—anything. Thankfully my friends heard that I thought about ending my own life and decided to hold an intervention with me. They not only told me how much they loved and appreciated me, they told me how much of an asshole I was and how rude I was to people. They wanted to be there for me but I was pushing them away. I then recognized I was projecting how I was feeling on others; I was doing to them what I felt was being done to me.

This intervention was a turning point for me. Things needed to change, but I had to change my mentality, my behaviors, and most of all my mind-set. From then on, my whole attitude changed and I really worked hard to make a difference in the community. I started going to more events, I started to get more involved, and then I became a member of Alpha Phi Alpha Fraternity, Inc. After joining my organization, I realized that I can achieve anything once I put my mind to it, which helped me build my confidence. College was definitely my breakthrough when it came to believing in myself.

What also pushed me was the mind-set to not give up. There are so many people out there who wished they could take advantage of opportunities in life. I *have* that opportunity so I am not going to squander it anymore. I will admit that I am still not fully over the situation, and there are people in my life that I know I just need to exit out of my life who do not add to the positive mind-set I need.

When we go through struggles, we falsely believe we are alone and that we are the only one going through difficulty, but there are so many people in the world who are also struggling—even worse than you are. So it is important to put that in perspective. This mind-set helps me to never give up and to always push through.

Having great people around you is key to helping you with your confidence, courage, and mind-set. As my friend

Michael Cadore suggested, having an ace partner or an accountability partner to keep you in check is important. We are our own worst critic, so to have someone bring us down to earth and remind us of the amazing person we are is vital for good mental and emotional health.

Celebrating the wins is important. Focus on what is going well in your life instead of dwelling on the negative. When was the last time you wrote down your goals and your dreams? I mean actually *wrote them down*? If you haven't, take some time to reflect on all that you wish to achieve and write it down. Determine what you can work on now, what are some short-term, mid-range, and long-term goals. Put the list somewhere you will be able to see it all the time. Eventually you will begin to develop timelines and action plans to achieve these goals and dreams. Some dreams may change with time, and that's okay too. I'm not where I was, thankfully—low-self-esteem and hating my life. I am headed for better things, and so are you.

Conclusion

Having confidence, courage, and a good mind-set is not easy; if it were easy then everyone would have it. I hope that these insights will inspire you to build your confidence up and will give you the courage to stick up for what is right and to have the mind-set to push through all challenges to greater heights. You are not alone in your struggles, so ask for help, seek guidance, and seek closure. Do not ever give up in achieving your dreams—if you want it, go and get it. Do not be afraid to fail. When things are getting tough, do not ever feel taking your life is the easy way out. As a wounded person, you do not realize how many other people in your life would be devastated if they lost you. Move on, push through, have a mentor or accountability partner, and continue to follow your dreams.

When you meet Edson O'Neale, you would you think he is a strong, confident person, but what you do not know is the demons of low self-worth that he has battled. He has previously gone through depression, thoughts of suicide, and a lack of self-confidence. There were times Edson thought this world would be better off without him, but because of the people he surrounds himself with and the will not to give up, he was able to push through. This will comes from his background and culture growing in the beautiful island of St. Croix, the U.S. Virgin Islands. His Trinidadian parents instilled a pride to always remember where you come from and who you are. That belief is what always keeps Edson going and giving back to his community.

The lightbulb finally came on in college where he realized his life matters and that he was destined to be an outstanding leader. He was involved in Student Government, Campus Activities, Student Organizations, and of course Greek Life. Edson crossed the burning sands of Alpha Phi Alpha Fraternity, Inc. in the spring of 2004 and never looked back. He served in several roles in the chapter such as Secretary Community Service Chair, Educational Chair, Vice President, and ultimately Chapter President. During his tenure as president, their organization won Fraternity of the Year, which was one of his proudest moments in college. Edson graduated with a degree in Sports Management from Saint Leo University in December of 2007. He furthered his education and went back to school in 2009 where he became a Graduate Assistant at Nova Southeastern University in programming. Working there, he realized his passion for working with students. He graduated with a Master of Science Degree in Leadership in December of 2010, and later came back home to Saint Leo University to work in Student Activities.

During his six and half years at Saint Leo University, he started off as the Assistant Director of Student Activities and then got promoted to the Director of Student Activities. Edson had the privilege of serving in many roles advising Student Government, the Campus Activities Board, Student Organizations, and Fraternity and Life. He also worked with leadership development, civic engagement, and the mascot team. Edson realized he had a story and wished to not only share it with students at Saint Leo, but with other students across the United States. Edson's background of getting bullied, having suicidal thoughts, and constantly questioning his self-worth will resonate with students. Edson wants students to know that they are not alone and you are worth more than you know.

More information: www.greekuniversity.org/edson

CHAPTER 11

Have You Trained Your Replacement Yet?

Michael Ayalon

I t happens all the time. You have a group of senior members of your fraternity or sorority that have the right experience on Executive Board to run the organization. They graduate, and they take all of that information with them. The effective recruitment techniques, the fundraising programs, the scholarship initiatives, the risk management procedures, and all the organizational memory is lost when they graduate, and the chapter is now lost as well.

What is the #1 problem that I see across fraternities and sororities that I work with all over North America? The answer is a lack of officer transition. We must work together to ensure a designated time each year that the outgoing Executive Board meets with the incoming Executive Board. A retreat away from campus, perhaps at a lake or a park, preferably where there are no internet connections available.

There needs to be an orderly transition where we share best practices, outline where we went wrong, highlight opportunities for the organization in the coming year, and share some things that could threaten our very existence. Every Fortune 500 company has a training program for new employees. Why is it that within fraternity and life, we throw new leaders into their positions without a formal training program and we wish them well? How is that a formula for success? As an organization, we must stress the importance of our officer transition retreat to our chapter, and designate that time as sacred time for the well-being of our chapter.

Why Leadership Matters

It's important to consider why students choose to be a leader in their organization. I often hear responses such as:

- building a résumé
- wanting to make an impact (change)
- seeking the respect of their peers
- nobody else wants to do it

When students get into that position of leadership, they often find it is difficult. The reasons for this difficulty vary:

- the time commitment that is needed
- they are the same age and have the same experience as the others in the organization
- everyone wants to go in different directions
- the stress that leadership positions usually bring

I hope you will seek out these leadership experiences in your organization, because if you do, it will serve you well in your career after college. While student apathy is probably something you are dealing with at the moment, I can assure you that the same problems will exist in the corporate world when you are put into a management role after graduation. If you can figure out how to motivate your fraternity/sorority chapter, you will have the ability to do the same thing in the corporate world. The key is knowing that everyone is motivated by something different, so you need to ask and find out exactly what motivates them.

By reading this book, you are a leader. As a leader, you must recognize that you only have some of the right answers. The other answers will come from the diverse members in your organization. While the temptation might be to do all the work yourself because you know it will be done the right way, you must fight this urge. It's important to share the workload and delegate to your organizational leaders. This way you won't burn out before the end of your term, and you're giving the necessary experience to other members of the organization so they will know how to lead when their time arrives. Recognize and reward them at chapter meetings for a job well done. Be sure to look ahead, plan, and notice the things that are happening around you. Sometimes you will need to change course. That is fine. You will also take (smart) risks, but when you make a mistake, you must own it and admit where you went wrong. Believe me, I have made a ton of mistakes while in college and throughout my career. It is because of those mistakes that I will succeed. You will too.

A Blueprint for Your Chapter

At this point, you might be wondering how you can take your chapter and turn it into the best chapter on campus, and perhaps the best chapter in the country for your organization. Chapters don't accidentally become the best. Instead, they plan for it by committing to the officer transition process to learn from past mistakes, not repeat those mistakes, and continuously improve their processes.

If we don't commit to effective officer transition, then we waste the chapter time and energy. We lose credibility with our own members, the university, and our local community. Suddenly the chapter progress has stopped and we are waiting for the guidance of a new leader. I have seen conflict and chaos emerge among the members, and this downward spiral of events can lead to chapter suspensions or a loss of the fraternity/sorority charter. It is that serious.

Train for the Future

It is your job to begin by identifying and training your future leaders. This ensures chapter longevity, creates a mentor relationship within the chapter, and creates an up-and-coming group of leaders that are ready to hit the ground running. You have benefited from your Greek affiliation. You have more skills today than when you came into the organization. Therefore, it is your responsibility to build the skills and leadership abilities of others in your chapter in areas such as leadership, finance, writing skills, public speaking skills, and fundraising. The good news is that you have plenty of resources available to you on a college campus. You have professors that can mentor your members, there are various networking organizations in your city, public speakers come to your university and your city on a regular basis, courses are available through the university, and your headquarters has leadership conferences that they arrange every year to ensure that your members have an opportunity for leadership development. Send your members and make that investment in your people.

| Evaluate Your Members

You should be evaluating all of your members as soon as they join the organization. What leadership position do they already hold in other organizations? What classes are they taking? What is their major/field of study? What kind of a student are they? What are their interests and future aspirations? What skills do they bring to the chapter? You should also revisit your files on each member prior to elections. Which member has the skills needed for this particular position that we are trying to fill? Your alumni and headquarters staff might have some ideas for you in this area. By doing a leadership inventory of your members, the answers will become clear as to who your future leaders will be. There are various assessments (some are free) to determine who has these skills, such as Myers-Briggs and DISC assessments. This information will help you in making decisions on who is right for which position, and that can lead to training opportunities well before any chapter election process.

In order to train these future leaders, place them in opportunities for increasing responsibility. Start with small chapter projects and see how they do. Expose them to other leaders on campus, such as other chapter leaders, council leaders, and campus leaders. Bring them to your meetings and explain that you are training future leaders to take your role one day, and that you expect that they will do an even better job in the future than you did. It is empowering to hear that from a current leader, so be sure to tell them often!

Plan an Officer Transition Retreat

You might be wondering what you can do to ensure this transition to new leadership is successful. First, be sure that your chapter is actively engaged in the transition process. You should attract qualified candidates to your chapter with the right skillsets. Have a job description prepared for each position, and screen all candidates with a list of questions that are designed to test their knowledge, ability, and desire for the position. We should review the progress made by the departing leadership, set meetings with all stakeholders (including campus, alumni, and headquarters), and then launch your new leadership team along with their vision and goals for the future. Once your leadership team is in place, a planned retreat for your leaders is vital in focusing on your chapter's goals and future.

Your officer transition retreat should contain the following agenda items:

1. Get a space for the meeting. Offsite, outside, on a lake, or in a park are all good ideas to get away

from the normal meeting spaces. This will limit your distractions!

2. Invite stakeholders to attend. Think about alumni, headquarters staff, and campus leaders.

3. SWOT assessment from the outgoing leadership and the incoming leadership. That stands for the chapter's strengths, weaknesses, opportunities, and threats.

4. Goals. They should be smart goals: **Specific, Measurable, Achievable, Relevant,** and **Time-based.**

5. One-on-one meetings by position between the outgoing and incoming leader.

6. Transfer documents, records, and programs.

7. Collect budgets and organizational calendar from the prior year.

8. Relay all best practices and failed initiatives.

9. Update any policies or bylaws.

10. Identify the future meetings that need to take place.

If you don't have an officer transition retreat, you will have no accountability, no regular events, hastily thrown together events, no up-and-coming leaders, senior members who are disengaged, a small handful of leaders that move the chapter forward, and burnout will be evident among your leadership. I would highly suggest that you make this officer transition retreat a part of your business plan to avoid these problems within your organization.

FROM LETTERS TO LEADERS

| Utilize Committees to Save Time

I want you to think about effective committee systems. How long is your chapter meeting? If you answered anything above sixty minutes, then I will tell you that you don't have an effective committee system. We shouldn't be arguing about what the recruitment T-shirts look like in a chapter meeting. It would be a waste of your chapter's time. If you are interested in having input in the recruitment T-shirt, the right time to provide that input would be during a recruitment committee meeting, which is separate from the chapter meeting. Also, your chapter vice president should be meeting with all the committee chairpersons BEFORE the chapter meeting. For example, the committee chairpersons could meet with the chapter vice president on a Friday, and then the chapter vice president can summarize everything for each committee at the chapter meeting on a Sunday. If that process is not currently happening, then it spills into your chapter meeting, and then the chapter meeting drags on for hours. Do not waste your members' time. Their time is precious, and so is yours.

Speaking of meetings, schedule your chapter meetings weekly. It should be happening on consistent times and days of the week. For example, every Sunday at 8 p.m. Your chapter has a Ritual for opening and closing meetings. Please use it! Your Ritual is what binds together the members of your chapter (and the alumni who are hopefully attending your meeting as well to advise the chapter). Be sure you have disseminated an agenda of your chapter meeting to all members at least two days prior to the meeting. That way your members will come prepared to discuss all the important matters. Be mindful to give jobs to each member of the organization during the meeting so that they are all engaged in the process, including senior members. Perhaps the senior members can tell us what they learned as a member of the organization and how that will help them moving forward. Each member should have a role to play in each meeting. This agenda will help you to stay on target, keep everyone engaged, get meaningful contributions from each member during the meeting, and be efficient in terms of your time.

One chapter that I visited told me that they don't allow new members into their chapter meetings because they didn't want the new members to see that occasionally brothers get into disagreements on the best way forward. Let me be very clear. It is normal for chapter members to disagree. However, we debate which way is the best way forward, and then we leave the meeting united in our direction as a brotherhood. It is incredibly important that your new members are involved in your meetings. They are your future leaders. Don't rob them of the time they need to build their understanding of how your organization runs, how they can contribute, and the amazing experience of democracy within today's fraternities and sororities. That piece is a critical piece of fraternity and sorority life, and it's critical if we want to retain our members. Why would we deny them that experience?

Communicate in Your Chapter and with Alumni

Communication is going to be the key to success for your chapter. You should be meeting with your Greek Life office at least twice per month, even if that's just to stop by the office and have an informal discussion with the Greek Advisor on your campus. Perhaps it's just to bring some them some coffee and donuts to reward them for their hard work and say thank you. You want and need a relationship with the people that work in this office. Should anything go wrong in your chapter, having a relationship in place with the administration BEFORE the incident will help you tremendously. This comes from experience.

You should have an ongoing relationship with your alumni and a designated representative of your chapter's alumni. You alumni have the resources you want, including time, money, and expertise. By engaging with a chapter director/advisor (or a rotation of alumni who come to your meetings each week), you will get needed expertise for your chapter and access to additional resources that the undergraduates cannot provide. It made our chapter significantly better, so if you don't have a chapter director/advisor, you should find one. There could be alumni in your area from another chapter; there could also be alumni in your area from another organization. Many of them would be honored to work with your chapter and help guide you. All you have to do is ask.

Your headquarters needs to know what your needs are, where you are excelling, and they can also share best practices from other chapters. Be sure to meet with them on a regular basis (this could be by phone or video conference if needed) to let them know how your chapter is progressing. They are paid to help you. Please engage with them and be honest about your needs. That way they can give you the information or resources you are seeking through one-on-one instruction or by developing programming for upcoming leadership conferences.

If anything should go wrong in your chapter that requires the immediate assistance of professionals such as a medical team or the police, call 911 immediately and get the authorities to help you. You should always cooperate with the police. Report all incidents that happen to your university, your headquarters, your chapter director, and other volunteers. Photos and videos could be useful later, so be sure to capture anything that happens on your cellphone for future use. Be sure to have a crisis management and communication plan with your headquarters and the university that everyone agrees with, and all chapter members should have that information readily available should the need arise.

By following this blueprint, you will be able to identify future leaders and properly train them to do their jobs. Hopefully, they will exceed your expectations and build on all of your successes. That is the goal. You want a chapter to come back to as an alumnus. You want future college students to have the same leadership opportunities that have been given to you. You want your son/daughter to join your organization and maybe even your chapter someday. This only happens when you have a plan and officer transition retreats are in place to ensure a proper handoff. Now get to work, start training your replacement, and let's continue to build a bigger and better tomorrow for fraternity and sorority life. I look forward to seeing what you can do!

Michael Ayalon, M.S.P., is the CEO of Greek University, an educational platform that has inspired countless institutions across North America in identifying, understanding, and resolving current social issues.

As a professional speaker, entrepreneur, and author, Mike has headlined over 400 presentations across 200 college campuses in 35 states to bring light on pressing problems, such as Sexual Assault Prevention, Hazing Prevention, Alcohol/Drug Abuse Prevention, and Motivation in Student Organizations. Mike's strong technological background and varied professional experience in helping to build companies from startup to over $25 million in annual sales gives him a profound understanding of the ways these issues penetrate all levels of corporate and educational structures today. His unique insight and hands-on approach enable him to create dynamic, positive, and results-driven keynotes and workshops that transform people's lives.

As a TIPS-certified trainer and the former Executive Director of Sigma Pi Fraternity with 120 chapters and over 100,000 members nationwide, Mike has a deep understanding of the current situation on campuses and corporations as well as a structured plan on how to empower our own youth to stop being a part of the problem and become an active part of its resolution. He is a member of the Association of Fraternity/Sorority Advisors, a programming partner for the North-American Interfraternity Council. In addition to his role with Greek University, Mike also currently serves as the Wilson County Rural Communities Opioid Response Coordinator through Middle Tennessee State University's Center for Health and Human Services. In conjunction with his role on the Board of Directors at DrugFree WilCo, Mike is actively reducing drug abuse and addiction in Middle Tennessee. Mike is a graduate of the School of Management at the University at Buffalo and has a master's degree from Cumberland University in public service management.

More information: www.greekuniversity.org/presentations

CHAPTER 12

Fraternity and Sorority Hazing: Exploring Precedent, Policy, and Practice

Dr. Jason L. Meriwether

ampus leaders are faced with an ever-evolving series of hazing cases often based on serious student injuries or death, and lawsuits that have implicated universities, local fraternity and sorority chapter members, national organizations, advisors, and university employees. Such hazing rituals have included mental abuse, financial extortion, severe violence, physical brutality, sleep-deprivation, binge drinking, consumption of hazardous foods or concoctions, psychological battery, alcohol or drug abuse, sexual battery, unhealthy sexual behaviors, emotional torment, blatant degradation, and death.

Fraternity and Sorority Life (FSL) professionals, advisors, and university administrators are often inundated with theories and ideas about how to stop hazing. This chapter encourages campus leaders to ensure that FSL professionals are appropriately resourced to combat hazing and to embrace preventive approaches to anti-hazing education and policies before a crisis or incident occurs. The text and recommendations will provide your leadership team with legally sound practices that protect students and the university. This chapter endeavors to provide pertinent approaches to align campus-wide hazing policies with educational tools that are rooted in trends supported by legal decisions rendered across the United States.

Hazing and Violence on Campus

Forms of mental and psychological hazing, such as high-stress situations or seemingly dangerous or harmful environments, are equally as dangerous as hazing that occurs through avenues of physicality, although they are frequently overlooked. Experts Colleen McGlone and George Schaefer further detailed the nature of psychological hazing, explaining,

> Types of psychological hazing may include verbal abuse, being subjected to highly stressful situations, being asked to perform acts that go against personal beliefs such as committing a crime, and/ or being subjected to a perceived physical danger. Another form of psychological

hazing includes simulating sexual activities. Psychological and physical hazing can occur separately or in conjunction with one another based upon the activities and the perspective of the person being hazed.[13]

Hank Nuwer defined the implicit and explicit nature of the phenomena, succinctly explaining, "Hazing involves a group's request (or the request of individuals within the group that the person in a subservient position perceives to be important) that a newcomer take some action in order to be held in esteem by the group and/or to gain entrance into an organization."[14]

Among definitive expressions of hazing within the context of university policy, Cornell University expressly stated:

To haze another person, regardless of the person's consent to participate. Hazing means an act that, as an explicit or implicit condition for initiation to, admission into, affiliation with, or continued membership in a group or organization, (1) could be seen by a reasonable person as endangering the physical health of an individual or as causing mental distress to an individual

---

[13]   Colleen McGlone and George R. Schaefer, "After the Haze: Legal Aspects of Hazing," *Entertainment and Sports Law Journal* 6, no. 1 (June 2008): 3; https://www.researchgate.net/publication/305308298_After_The_Haze_Legal_Aspects_of_Hazing.

[14]   Hank Nuwer, *Wrongs of Passage: Fraternities, Sororities, Hazing, and Binge Drinking* (Bloomington, IN: Indiana University Press, 1999), 37.

through, for example, humiliating, intimidating, or demeaning treatment, (2) destroys or removes public or private property, (3) involves the consumption of alcohol or drugs, or the consumption of other substances to excess, or (4) violates any University policy.[15]

James P. Barber stated, "Many students feel a need to establish a culture of exclusion, for which hazing is the entry, in an attempt to create smaller communities and fashion a student culture over which they have control."[16] Still, institutions should mitigate the perceived value of establishing such subcultures. Darby Dickerson defined the issue of hidden harm within student subcultures, stating, "College administrators should continue to send strong and regular anti-hazing messages. . . . We must help students understand that activities they perceive to be either fun or a revered tradition are deadly."[17]

---

[15] https://scl.cornell.edu/get-involved/campus-activities/organization-registration/hazing#:~:text=HAZING%3A%20To%20haze%20another%20person,the%20person's%20consent%20to%20participate.

[16] James P. Barber, "Ever After Strictly and Rigidly Obeyed—with Some Exceptions: Administrative Responses to Hazing in the 1870s," *The Research Journal of the Association of Fraternity/Sorority Advisors* 7, no. 4 (Spring 2012):121.

[17] Darby Dickerson, "Prescription for Disaster: The Problem of 'Hidden Harms' and Hazing," *Campus Activities Programming* 41, no. 6 (Jan./Feb. 2009): 13.

As Walter Kimbrough postulated,

> The challenge I and others engaged in
> this work have is that every three years
> or so, there is a new group that has not
> heard about the risks but know all about
> the traditions. Today's students don't
> know about Joel Harris, Michael Davis,
> Joseph Green, Kenitha Saafir, or Kristin
> High. They all died trying to belong.
> They also don't know about the dozens
> more injured every year, and the hundreds
> who will have emotional scars from their
> experiences. They know they want to
> belong and that means pledging—illegal
> or not. So the cycle has started again.
> We are on the clock—five years or so
> to change the culture or watch another
> young person die.[18]

Caroline Keating and others in the Department of Psychology
at Colgate University extensively discussed hazing practices
and initiation rituals among undergraduate students in Greek
Letter Organizations (GLOs) and among student athletes.
They explained that "initiations provide early opportunities
for group leaders to establish power over newcomers to the
organization" and they defined initiation rituals to be inclusive
of "activities perceived to be fun and rewarding, physically
and emotionally demanding, embarrassing, socially deviant,

---

[18] Walter Kimbrough, "Last Word—Black Greek Deathwatch," *Diverse
Education* (February 10, 2010), https://diverseeducation.com/article/13515/.

degrading, painful, and sometimes dangerous or brutal."[19] Initiation rituals include adherence to very prescriptive traditions within the group that may include clearly assigned and defined roles for established members, to the end of repeating experiences of current members. Keating explained that in these instances the initiation process is rationalized by the concept that initiates are on a path to being better and more productive members of the group. Keating delineated the aims of certain types of rituals in detail, noting,

> Certain types of initiation activities seem orchestrated to achieve particular effects. Experiencing physical extremes may train initiates to withstand physical duress. Engaging in social deviance may primarily function to etch distinction between the in-group and normative groups in the minds and emotions of initiates. Maltreatment may elicit cognitive, behavioral, and emotional symptoms of social dependency. From a functional perspective, different types of initiation experiences seem designed to preserve group features and cultivate group allegiance in particular ways.[20]

---

[19] Caroline F. Keating, Jason Pomerantz, Stacy D. Pommer, Samantha J. H. Ritt, Lauren M. Miller, and Julie McCormick, "Going to College and Unpacking Hazing: A Functional Approach to Decrypting Initiation Practices among Undergraduates," *Group Dynamics: Theory, Research, and Practice* 9, no. 2 (2005): 105, 107.

[20] Ibid., 106.

Liability vs. Lawsuits: Examining Critical Legal Precedent

In an article for ACPA (American College Personnel Association) in 2015, I discuss legal issues and lawsuits involving universities, advisors, and Greek Letter Organizations, noting, "student conduct professionals can glean many lessons from such court cases and the resulting court decisions."[21] Beyond student conduct, I later provide in my book, *Dismantling Hazing in Greek-Letter Organizations*, a substantive review of higher education case law as it relates to hazing prevention, noting, "to combat hazing, colleges and universities need to address it in legal, social, and educational contexts."[22] Accordingly, it is important to consider the impact of a series of cases that provide guidance for university leaders. "Colleges and universities face increased levels of liability when prior organizational behavior, or a history of hazing on the campus, is considered by the courts."[23]

University leaders must be cognizant of how history factors into liability. In particular, reasonable foresight is established in *Knoll v. Board of Regents of the University of Nebraska* (1999) which involves a hazing incident within the Phi Gamma Delta Fraternity. A student who was pledging the local chapter of Phi Gamma Delta was kidnapped and

---

[21] James L. Meriwether, "Training versus Trials: Educative Strategies to Mitigate Hazing Liability," ACPA (June 2015), https://www.myacpa.org/entity/commission-student-conduct-legal-issues/blog/training-versus-trials-educative-strategies.

[22] James L. Meriwether, *Dismantling Hazing in Greek-Letter Organizations: Effective Practices for Prevention, Response, and Campus Engagement* (Washington, DC: NASPA, 2020), 60.

[23] Ibid., 74.

beaten, eventually being handcuffed to a bathroom radiator. Attempting to escape the bathroom, the student fell through a window and suffered severe injuries. This led to a suit claiming University negligence due to failing to adequately enforce hazing policies and policies governing the use of alcohol on campus. After summary dismissal by the lower court, the state's supreme court established critical precedent for reasonable foresight, noting that the university was aware of issues of hazing on campus involving other organizations. Further, the state supreme court was aware of specific incidents of hazing involving the fraternity in this matter. Based on these two factors, the court's decision explained that the University should have reasonably foreseen acts of hazing by the local chapter of Phi Gamma Delta.

Beyond issues of reasonable foresight, precedent also demonstrates the importance of a chapter advisor in the process of educating local members about the risks and dangers of hazing. Describing the need for substantive engagement by chapter advisors in my book, I state: "People in this role are still required to comply with university standards and policies designed to prevent hazing. Failure by advisors to comply with education standards can have adverse consequences."[24] Advisors also face the risk of personal liability by failing to actively engage their chapter members as part of the preventative process to educate students about the risks and dangers of hazing. This risk is evidenced by *Kenner v. Kappa Alpha Psi Fraternity* (2002), which involved violent beatings and torture by members of the fraternity against a University of Pittsburgh student who was pledging

---

[24] Ibid., 63.

the local chapter. The resulting lawsuit was filed against the university, a number of University of Pittsburgh employees, fraternity members, the chapter advisor, and the local and national chapter. Upon appeal, the results of *Kenner v. Kappa Alpha Psi Fraternity* (2002) placed liability upon the fraternity advisor while all other defendants in the case were dismissed by the court. Specifically, the advisor had not discussed the university's hazing policies with the chapter, failed to ensure that chapter members reviewed organizational rules and regulations about hazing, and did not provided information regarding the risks, dangers, or sanctions for breaking the rules and policies regarding hazing and violence. University leaders should develop robust avenues for advisor training that involves advisors, current chapter members, and aspiring members.

> Any such training is ineffective if it involves simple, nondescript sessions that do not address the specific requirements of prohibitive campus regulations, organizational policies, and state laws. Further, student affairs professionals must continually share this information with campus stakeholders and update their policies accordingly.[25]

Beyond training for advisors, it is necessary for universities to establish and sustain practices for education, training, and clear reporting options regarding hazing. Following beatings and torturous hazing activities levied against a Texas

---

[25] Ibid., 71.

A&M university Corps of Cadets drill team member, the victim's family filed a lawsuit against a plethora of university employees, the drill team advisor, and student drill team leaders (*Alton v. Texas A&M University*, 1999). In both the original complaint and appeal, officials of Texas A&M and all Corps of Cadet leaders were dismissed from the case and granted immunity by the courts. According to the court, university leaders had overseen and delivered reasonable education for their campus about the risks and dangers of hazing through parent and student orientation, provision of written brochures and materials, and for establishing pathways to report any concerns or allegations related to hazing (*Alton v. Texas A&M University*, 1999).

The argument of solidifying practices for consistent and robust training, commitment to educative approaches to hazing prevention, and provision of clear policies and avenues to report hazing is furthered by *Lloyd v. Alpha Phi Alpha Fraternity, Inc.* (1999). Cornell University transfer student Sylvester Lloyd was violently brutalized and also tortured psychologically by the local fraternity chapter. Following the lawsuit, the case dismissed because Cornell University had published anti-hazing policies that were published and clarified the risks and dangers of hazing along with other university materials. Accordingly, there was no promise or implied contract of protection for Mr. Lloyd or other students. The court notes that because the local chapter did not have a history of hazing, there was no issue of reasonable foresight, and once the campus leadership became aware of the policy violation, it was immediately resolved by following the university's hazing policy.

Recommendations for Effective Practice

Compulsory Education Requirements

No chapter should be permitted to engage in any intake, rush, or new member activities without participation in a required educative course that explores the risks, dangers, hidden harms, and liabilities associated with hazing. Participants should include aspiring members, active chapter members, campus and local advisors, and representation from the national organization or graduate chapter with oversight for the campus. These sessions should include review of all campus and organizational policies, relevant state laws, sanctions for violating policies and applicable laws, and pathways to report hazing. All participants should sign documents to verify receipt, review, and comprehension of all information provided.

Provided Substantive Advisor Training

It is critical for campus leaders to engage advisors beyond providing signatures for events or chaperoning actives. Training for advisors should be conducted by campus FSL professionals, national experts on hazing prevention, or by other experienced advisors. Campus leaders should create annual certificates to demonstrate completion of requisite training and set standards for renewal of required training on an annual basis. Such training should include campus advisors and graduate chapter or national advisors. Failure to certify or re-certify by advisors should result in revocation of privilege of local chapters to take new members.

Discuss Hazing During New Student and Parent Orientation

Orientation is a critical point to address hazing, particularly for organizations that allow first-time freshman to become members of local chapters. Orientation must extend beyond course scheduling, bill payment, social activities, or college transitions discussions. Introducing parents and families to the risks and dangers of hazing provides another layer of education to help reduce risk of harm.

Resolve Issues of Reasonable Foresight Recordkeeping

Campus leaders must curate historical data and empower chapter advisors and FSL professionals with accurate and adequate records of campus hazing. Chapters that have a history of hazing may require additional monitoring, weightier requirements for allowing new membership, and additional advisement from their national organization.

Acknowledge Hidden Harms

Professors Elizabeth Allan and Mary Madden[26] and Darby Dickerson[27] discuss the lack of understanding and sometimes outright failure to acknowledge that hazing is dangerous. As part of any educative approach to hazing prevention, it is prudent for campus leaders to discuss the notion of hidden harms by exploring other hazing cases that have involved serious injury or death due to drinking, brutality, or attempts

---

[26] For their full article "Hazing in View: College Students at Risk" (March 11, 2008), see https://www.stophazing.org/wp-content/uploads/2014/06/hazing_in_view_web1.pdf.

[27] Dickerson, "Prescription for Disaster," https://papers.ssrn.com/sol3/papers.cfm?abstract_id=1336697.

to uphold chapter traditions in spite of the potential danger to aspiring members of sororities and fraternities. As part of any mandatory education activity prior to intake of new members, discussion about hidden harms or perceptions that risky activities are not dangerous is prudent.

Conclusion

The cases and recommendations described above are shared to prompt readers to move beyond the simple approach of condemning hazing or positioning hazing as campus taboo. It is critical to establish anti-hazing policies, have honest and consistent discussions with students about the dangers and risks of becoming involved with hazing, establish a clear channel for reporting complaints, and to address issues of reasonable foresight when chapters or campus communities have a history of hazing. Taking a proactive and vigilant approach to prevent hazing requires consistent and sustained engagement. Doing so reduces risk and increases the chance of preventing harm to another student due to senseless hazing and violence.

Dr. Jason L. Meriwether is an experienced higher education leader with over two decades of service to public and private universities. Jason is editor of the book *Dismantling Hazing in Greek-Letter Organizations: Effective Practices for Prevention, Response, and Campus Engagement*. He is a financially active member of Alpha Phi Alpha Fraternity, Inc. and has conducted education workshops for numerous Interfraternity Council (IFC), National Pan-Hellenic Council (NPHC), National Panhellenic Conference (NPC), National Asian Pacific Islander Desi American Panhellenic Association (NAPA), and National Association of Latino Fraternal Organizations, Inc. (NALFO) chapters, in addition to multiple multicultural, service, honors, and music fraternities and sororities. Jason's national presentations on legal issues related to hazing have been the subject of cover stories in the *Student Affairs Today* newsletter and in *College Athletics and The Law*, and he has been featured on CNN's

"Headline News" as a national expert on fraternity and sorority hazing. As an advocate for community engagement, over 15,000 documented hours of volunteerism, service, and mentoring has been completed by sororities and fraternities under his leadership. Jason earned a PhD in Educational Administration with a specialization in Higher Education Leadership at Indiana State University and currently serves Humboldt State University as Vice President of Enrollment Management.

More information: www.greekuniversity.org/jason

CHAPTER 13

Speaking Your Truth, Taking Up Space, and Being Fully Present

Tish Norman

There I was—a spry, young freshman, sitting at my first college Step Show. My roommate/cousin and our neighbors sat in the bleachers in our university's gymnasium. It was the early '90s. It was Homecoming Week, and the energy was off the chain!

Students, parents, professors, alumni, both young and seasoned were hugging, laughing, smiling, and huddled in anticipation for the show to begin. The sea of people consisted of leather jackets, ensembles dawning the school colors, sweatshirts with the school's mascot, and colorful Greek letters that seemed to leap off the jackets right toward you.

You know what a Step Show is, right? I am not referring to a Stroll Competition or Yard Show, but a traditional competitive Black Greek Step Show. Before Black Greek-letter organizations (BGLOs) started infusing pre-recorded videos, elaborate props, voiceovers, up lights, and smoke machines in their performances, there was a time when this performative culture, exclusive to BGLOs, was absolute. Simple. Unfiltered. There were steppers and a stage.

Through the years, BGLOs developed distinct personalities and styles. Some fraternities slide, glide, and almost drift as they stroll. Others stomp and clap with large and powerful movements. Some prefer precision or slight, more fluid shifts in bodies, while others hop and leap, similar to calisthenics. Each has hand signs, calls, and colors distinct to them, so the culture and tradition is very vibrant. For over sixty years, BGLOs have used Step Shows to fundraise, sing chants about their history, to showcase their creativity, and to celebrate brotherhood and sisterhood. One of the best features at any celebratory BGLO gathering, like a Step Show is the proverbial "Roll Call." This occurs when the emcee "takes attendance."

Sequentially, each organization is announced. They stand or stay seated, signifying with their respective chant, unique call and response, and hand signs. Though brief, it is very exciting, as organizations showcase for approximately thirty seconds with massive enthusiasm, cheers, or jeers from the audience.

Fast-forward to my first opportunity to participate in a Roll Call. I was too excited! When the emcee called our organization's name, my chapter stood up and we represented! That is exactly what a Greek Roll Call is—it demonstrates giving voice, being fully present, and that you take up space.

In the same way, as the world struggles with unprecedented divide, overlapping crises—a global health pandemic and its accompanying economic fallout, a global response to centuries of systematic racism and police brutality against Black Americans, and millions of job losses—for my literary contribution, I have chosen to optimistically focus on the glass being half full. I have chosen to charge the readers to answer the Roll Call. When we heal and move forward from this dark time in American history, we will look back at 2020 and the era of COVID-19 and say, "Our chapter made it through, our bonds are stronger, and we *still* have so much to express gratitude for."

Join me as I combine the academic staple of a budding scholar, my firsthand experience as a Fraternity/Sorority Life (FSL) speaker, and the interaction of your favorite blog so we can show out when we answer the Roll Call!

Speaking Your Truth: How to Lead Through Change

Change is inevitable. The word alone elicits a gamut of emotions from those who hear it. Some welcome change. They thrive on seeking opportunities to explore the unknown, to imagine, reimagine, and to search for territories not yet chartered. For others, it strikes fear in their hearts. They panic. The anxiety of the unknown, deviating them from the familiar, shakes them to their core. Most of us lie somewhere in that gray area, safely nestled in our routines, mixed with random adventures of the unknown.

One thing I know for sure, the only thing in life that is guaranteed is change.

There is a lot happening right now. Coronavirus has changed the world permanently. Climate change is happening across the globe. Millions of students got homeschooling that they did not sign up for. Amazon revolutionized the way we shop, crayons now come in colors that reflect melanated people around the world, and America's political landscape is battered, bruised, and dangerously divided. No matter how one feels about change, we know that it happens and if 2020 did not teach us anything else, we know change happens by the minute.

In the same way, when change happens in your chapter, how do you lead through change? Do you acquiesce? Do you suffer in silence? Do you argue? Are you a passive-aggressive communicator? Are you passive during the meeting, then have a meeting after the meeting? If you do either of these, how is that working out for you? Consider this. We are natural innovators of change. In order to lead and inspire *through* change, one must speak their truth and speak up. Communication is key. Leaders must realize their influence on others. Influence is the vehicle in which change is possible and your chapter is waiting for you to take the lead. Leaders have double duty. Leaders reach forward toward new horizons and reach back to bring others along, leading by example. Leaders don't pull the ladder up once they climb to the top; they leave it there for someone else to climb.

Having the ability to inspire others to action is an important skill to have when doing the work of your chapter. Honestly, it is critical to some chapters' mere survival.

Here are a few recommendations to help you lead through change:

- Call a Line Brother to catch up, connect, and strategize.
- Schedule a 60-minute fireside chat with other council presidents—just to share, think, and inspire one another.
- Address current challenges, and discuss over a veggie pizza.
- Reach out to your Littles and encourage them to become leaders.
- Leverage the talent in your chapter.
- Conduct a skills inventory to discover the strengths within your group.
- Take a walk or run outside with a few brothers and sisters.
- Check in on chapter officers. How are they communicating with members? Make necessary recommendations.
- Comment on their posts with positive remarks.

Dr. Myles Monroe said, "The test of true leadership is when the leadership principles are upheld in the absence of that leader." Read that quote again. Let it sink in. Ultimately, leading through change takes open, honest, consistent effective communication that moves people to action. Encourage all chapter members to work. Speak your truth; even when it may seem uncomfortable.

This idea of speaking your truth as you lead through change can be a fundamental principle of your chapter. Change isn't easy. The reality is change is a disruptor. The ebbs and flows of uncertainty can most definitely lead to anxiety. So, when you accept that change is going to happen and that it cannot be avoided, we must practice a flexible, adaptable, and adjustable mind-set. Change on your campus and within your organization now, will prepare you for the change you will face in your career. You will continue to develop and sharpen these skills as you learn to accept change—lean into it, and not flee from it. Make a promise to yourself before you graduate to leave your organization different and better. Leave a legacy of responding positively to change so others will be encouraged to do the same.

Reflect & Apply

List two ways speaking your truth can help you lead through change in your chapter, virtually and in-person:

1. _____

2. _____

Taking Up Space: Fostering Intentionally Inclusive Environments

After an organization or company produces a major event, members of the planning committee gather to debrief. At these meetings, discourse about successes, setbacks, areas of improvement, what went well and areas to pay a bit more attention to takes place. The team works to identify strategies that were most effective, ensuring that the original objectives, goals, and learning outcomes were met. And if not, how do we adjust, pivot, and hit the target for the next event.

These debriefs are important because they allow groups to assess, plan, implement progress strategies, promote growth, and encourage forward movement amongst its members. In the wake of a year that will live in infamy, not to preclude the past, how has your chapter responded to the needs of its members? Have you debriefed? What conversations, activities, and events has your organization sponsored that addresses this current turbulent climate?

Diversity, equity, and inclusion (DEI) are not just hot topics across professional industries, but on campuses as well. Identifying and recruiting top leaders on campus as potential new members is good for your organization—and yet, diverse demographics often find "themselves" absent, vastly underrepresented or under-engaged in collegiate programmatic spaces.

FSL sends powerful messages when they demonstrate a commitment to DEI work that is fueled by action, not just rhetoric. Embracing people from all kinds of backgrounds and having the courage to have the critical conversations show that equity is important, as it helps foster an inclusive campus culture. Remember, diversity is not just cultural or ethnic differences. It's economic status, education level, experiential, familial, age, and a plethora of other categories. As communities that stand out on campus, all eyes are on you.

You are uniquely poised to seize opportunities to educate yourselves and your chapter by supporting inclusive initiatives that celebrate our differences. For example, in my state of residence, the University of Georgia has broken ground on the installation of campus stone markers to recognize the nine historically Black fraternities and sororities that make up the National Pan-Hellenic Council (NPHC). Similar projects have been launched at numerous other institutions across the country, including the University of Florida, University of Tennessee, and the University of North Carolina – Chapel Hill. Why does this matter? Many white fraternities and sororities live in houses, commonly known as "Fraternity Row." You can drive down a street on campus and see huge homes dawning Greek letters from white fraternities and sororities, but seldom does one see the same for BGLOs.

What distinguishes majority Greeks from NPHC, for instance, is how they are symbolically represented on campus. Predominantly white institutions, PWIs, traditionally, do not have "plots." That custom began at historically Black colleges and universities, HBCUs, in the late 1960s. However, projects like the aforementioned will support ongoing efforts to create a more welcoming and inclusive environment, giving opportunity to recognize our historically Black fraternities and sororities in this meaningful way.

As leaders, you determine the course of your chapter. In order to foster and sustain inclusive environments, it is crucial that you be intentional with your programs and prioritize taking up space where everyone feels respected, informed, and understood. Debrief. Then regroup, refocus, recap, review, reinvent, and revamp, if necessary.

Reflect & Apply

What are two ways you can begin encouraging your chapter to be more intentional when planning future programming or supporting other councils' events?

1. _____
   _____
2. _____
   _____

Being Fully Present: Relevant Programming That Makes a Difference

Edutainment was the fourth album from Boogie Down Productions, a '90s Hip Hop group hailing from the Bronx, New York. Because of the prolific writing and dope rhyming skills, referred to by many today as "bars," from rapper KRS-One, he delivered to Hip Hop a very socially conscious masterpiece to his audience. As Hip-Hop's self-proclaimed "Teacher," KRS-One created an unprecedented marriage between education and entertainment. Released on August 7, 1990, the year 2020 marked the 30th anniversary of *Edutainment*, reminding the music world and *real* Hip Hop fans of BDPs cultural influence and impact.

In the same way, fraternities and sororities can follow suit. It's not "either or," it is "both and." Programming has two sides—it is fun *and* you learn something. Programs are events that are sponsored by students, like a programming board, or events sponsored by the university for the benefit of students. In college we grow, transform, experience joys, disappointments, victories, failures, sadness, happiness, cry tears of joy or pain, learn and unlearn—all to the good of becoming who will eventually be. We leave college drastically different from how we entered and that, in part, is due to programs that enhance skills as student leaders and help students feel a sense of belonging and community.

Does your organization's programming include these experiences? Is your chapter fully present during planning and execution? Do we see five members at the food drive and thirty-two at the party? Is there partial attendance at the *planning* of Homecoming, New Member Mingle/Meet the Greeks, Ritual Celebration Week, Hazing Prevention Week, and Social Justice work, and Greek Week, but full attendance *at* the actual event?

College is an appetizer for the real world, and actively participating in FSL, if applied correctly, augments your personal development. Why not take advantage of your advantages! Simply put, as part of a larger community, FSL naturally fosters the ability for advanced self-development.

Members have the opportunity to work across councils and with other campus organizations in planning programs with diverse groups. Do like KRS-One, make it social *and* educational. Keep it well-rounded, memorable, and creative. The year 2020 taught us that we should express gratitude for what we have and to unleash our creativity to make things happen.

Unleash your creativity. Attend the next planning meeting with ten cool ideas to present to the committee. Tap into your innovative side. Research. See what fellow chapters are doing at other campuses, reimagine that event, and customize it for your campus. Bring back an oldie but goodie. Find out what your chapter did in the '80s or '90s. Revamp it and launch. Oh, you're living in the best of times and the worst of times, where information develops and disseminates at the speed of thought! It is time to answer the Roll Call in your programmatic efforts.

"Hold on!" "It's not that easy, Tish. I am already bogged down." "Members do not show up like they need to." "What should I do? There are only a few of us that keep things moving." Well, I am glad you asked. When I was an undergrad, my university scheduled midterms right before Homecoming. What? Are you serious? Before joining my sorority, that meant going to the library before going to the party. I had to apply a wicked amount of self-discipline in order to attend parties and activities happening every night of Homecoming week. Once I joined my sorority, it got real! Can you relate?

If this struggle of balancing a demanding schedule and getting your chapter to be "fully present" sounds familiar, here is where FSL has the opportunity to cultivate or to continue supporting impactful programs that your chapter sponsors. Consider the following:

- Re-emphasize that the core values of your chapter and FSL membership requires continuing education, supporting social/emotional intelligence, officer training, and leadership development.

- Relevant programming is an expectation of FSL members to sponsor and support. Add a little spice to the format in which your chapter acknowledges and rewards relevant and impactful programming. Emphasize organizations that included activities like: anti-hazing, social justice, alcohol education, improving faculty relations, equity and multiculturalism, tolerance, gender issues, sexual assault, health education, scholarship, critical thinking, and fundraising.

- Commit to fun programs that render strength and stability to the larger community and offer relevant learning opportunities that support the shared values espoused by your chapter, national organization, and FSL.

It is time to answer the Roll Call. Represent. Show up— fully. Take up space. Reignite your chapter's energy and make a difference. Move all the pettiness aside. Nobody has time for that. Speak your truth and speak up. The world needs it. Your campus needs it. Be intentional in your efforts of change. When you and your chapter need a massive dose of motivation, crack this book open and remember what applied to you the most. Remember what you learned in this chapter and share it with others. Smile! Stand up. "Say it with your chest!" Let the people know that your chapter is present, ready, and poised for world-class leadership.

Reflect & Apply

How can I personally support my chapter in gaining the skills that influence their environments, and fosters safe and meaningful experiences within their organization?

1. _____
   _____

2. _____
   _____

Tish Norman is a native of Cleveland, Ohio, and is the Executive Director of Transforming Leaders Now, Inc., an educational consulting company specializing in college and career readiness, women's leadership, and the African-American experience.

Tish started her career in the classroom in Cincinnati, Ohio, teaching 3rd and 4th grade, and after being crowned Miss Black Cincinnati, she decided to take her gifts to Hollywood. Commercials, music videos, game shows, documentaries, sitcoms, Tish did it all!

Now, almost twenty years later, as a professional speaker and having delivered over 1,000 presentations, Tish's unparalleled energy, delivery style, and stirring keynotes have become favorites among universities, associations, and leadership conferences from coast to coast.

Tish is a contributing author of several articles and three books, *From Mediocre to Magnificent*, *Leading the Way*, and *#BLACKOUT: Real Issues and Real Solutions to Real Challenges Facing Black Student Affairs Professionals*.

A graduate of Kentucky State University, Tish has a master's in education from Pepperdine University and is a doctoral pursuant in Pan-African Studies, where her research focuses on memory and the Black sorority.

Having spoken in forty-five states and fourteen countries and despite her rigorous academic obligations, Tish still maintains an active speaking schedule, keynoting at dozens of campuses and leadership conferences every year. Tish currently resides in Atlanta.

More information: www.greekuniversity.org/tish

Call to Action

Inaction breeds doubt and fear. Action breeds confidence and courage. If you want to conquer fear, do not sit home and think about it. Go out and get busy.—Dale Carnegie

Now we have reached the point in the book where you need to determine the end of this story. I hope these chapters have inspired you. I hope our team has stretched your imagination and revealed the importance of student leadership on your college campus. What role will you play in making your campus and your organization the best it can possibly be?

We have given you the blueprint for a better community. However, the house will not get built unless you pick up a hammer. Remember, the community around you will know who you are and what you value based on your actions, not your words. It is not good enough to stand in the front of the room and repeat your creed or motto each week without taking the matching actions to demonstrate that you are truly living those words. Remind the others around you what they committed to. Ask them to join you in making a difference, even if we start with something small.

It reminds me of the story of the man who lived in a home with a beautiful view of the ocean. Each morning he would wake up at 6 a.m. and look out at the waves crashing down on the sand just outside of his home. Every morning he watched as a young woman would walk the beach. This woman would find a starfish that had been pushed ashore, and then she would throw the starfish back into the ocean. It seemed endless, but she did that for all the starfish that she found washed ashore that day.

Over the next few days, the same exact scene repeated itself. Finally, at the end of the week, the man walked out on the beach to greet the young woman at 6 a.m.

"Why do you do this every day?" asked the man.

"What do you mean?" said the young woman.

"Each morning I see you throw these starfish back into the ocean. You do this for hours. It will never end. The starfish will continue to get washed up on shore every day. It won't ever make a difference," said the man.

The young woman picked up one starfish sitting on the sand below them and threw it into the ocean. "Well, it just made a difference for that starfish," said the young woman.

Will you make a difference on your campus? If so, I invite you to join me. Send me an email at <u>bookings@greekuniversity. org</u> to share how you are making a difference in your community. You can also learn more about our educational programming on our website at <u>www.greekuniversity.org</u>. Our speakers are ready to work with your chapter, your council, your fraternity/sorority community, your athletics team, your student organization, or all students on campus to help inspire your community, grow your community, and make it a safer place for all students.

Wishing you all the best in your leadership journey.

Michael Ayalon

Made in the USA
Middletown, DE
04 June 2024

55252050R00104